Angels
Alliance with Beings of Light
By Luiz Santos

Copyright © 2022 Luiz Santos
All rights reserved.
No part of this book may be reproduced in any form or by any means without written permission from the copyright holder.
Cover image © Orbis Studio
Review by Marco Avelar
Graphic design by Tania Navarro
Layout by Paulo Xavier
All rights reserved to:
Luiz A. Santos
Category: Holism

VELLAZ

Summary

Prologue 5
Chapter 1 Angels 8
Chapter 2 Guardian Angels 15
Chapter 3 Preparing for the Ritual 22
Chapter 4 Energy Cleansing 30
Chapter 5 Intention in Ritual 37
Chapter 6 Meditation for Angelic Connection 44
Chapter 7 Visualization and Tuning 51
Chapter 8 Basic Invocation 58
Chapter 9 Incense and Herbs for Connection 65
Chapter 10 Crystals for Angelic Communication 72
Chapter 11 Angelic Altar 79
Chapter 12 Symbols and Signs 86
Chapter 13 The Language of Angels 93
Chapter 14 Prayer and Its Strength in Connection 100
Chapter 15 Identifying Presence 108
Chapter 16 Gratitude Ritual 116
Chapter 17 Seeking Guidance in Dreams 123
Chapter 18 Angels and the Lunar Cycle 130
Chapter 19 Strengthening the Connection 137
Chapter 20 Connecting with the Personal Guardian Angel 142
Chapter 21 Angelic Protection for Home and Family 148
Chapter 22 The Role of Archangels in Rituals 155
Chapter 23 Channeling Messages 162
Chapter 24 Angelic Visions 169
Chapter 25 Healing Rituals 177

Chapter 26 Strengthening the Energy Field 183
Chapter 27 Ritual for Requests 188
Chapter 28 Personal Spiritual Journey 193
Chapter 29 Angelic Wisdom 198
Chapter 30 The Circle of Light: Protection and Spiritual Strengthening 204
Chapter 31 State of Union with Angels 210
Chapter 32 Concluding the Cycle 217
Epilogue 223

Prologue

Quiet your heart, for this is a moment of discovery. Not every day does the veil that separates the visible from the invisible open with such generosity. In your hands is a silent calling, an invitation that resonates from a dimension only accessible to those with an open spirit. In this journey of words and revelations, these pages become doors, each concept a key. There was no mere chance that brought you here but rather a subtle purpose, an inexplicable attraction to what has always existed, even beyond understanding.

Here, the path is not made of theories, but of presences that speak in silence. Beings of light, transcending time and space as we know it, are all around you. They walk among us as invisible guides, extending their light and protection to those who, perhaps unknowingly, seek them. Such a presence overcomes fear and fills the soul with lasting serenity—a touch that no human eye could see and no word could fully describe. Yet, here, you will find the touch of a greater world.

Beyond the limits of this plane, angels, the guardians and messengers of the divine, are energies that shape reality, guiding and protecting. They know the deepest corners of your existence, from shadows to the brightest lights, from moments of despair to sparks of hope. In every step that has brought you here, these beings watched you with patience and care, waiting for the moment when your consciousness could finally receive them.

In opening this book, you allow these sacred lights to draw closer. Within each page, each symbol, lies more than mere words. They are portals, silent invitations for your mind and heart to walk in the elevated frequency where angels dwell. You will feel along this path that each thought, each intention, is a step toward understanding and harmony with the whole. There exists a language that only the heart comprehends, and within these pages, this language will reveal itself.

Angels, in their essence, are not distant figures or mystical entities that reside in unreachable heavens; they are realities surrounding us with gentleness. Their missions go beyond mere protection; they illuminate the shadows we all carry, offering clarity in moments of doubt. Sometimes, they send subtle signs—a warmth wrapping around you for no apparent reason, a sense of peace descending when fear insists. Other times, they show symbols—a feather found by chance or a sequence of numbers that repeats—a mystery intended to capture your attention, reminding you of the sacred connection that never fades.

Each chapter draws you into a universe that celebrates angelic presence. And beyond the words lies a unique vibration, a field of energy inviting you to open your heart, expand your soul, and listen to that which is not heard with the ears, but felt at the core of your being. It is a frequency that, as you attune, resonates with the angels and allows them to be consciously by your side—not only as guardians but as companions on a journey leading to the very understanding of the divine.

This book is not just for reading; it is a ritual of opening. As you turn its pages, a field of light forms around you, an extension of the angels' divine messages. It is as if each page is a new wave of connection, carrying you a bit further, a bit deeper, toward a truth that only the heart can fully grasp. You are about to unveil the mystery that has always been with you, a presence that, though invisible, has always protected and guided you.

The answers you have perhaps sought for so long may not present themselves linearly or logically but will find you here, within words that reveal ancient secrets. Open your mind and release your preconceptions about existence. This book is a reminder that you have never been alone and that each experience has, in fact, been a preparation for this very moment to manifest. The journey begins here, and as you journey through its pages, you will perceive that the alliance with beings of light is, and has always been, closer than you could have ever imagined.

Chapter 1
Angels

In the shadows between worlds, there is a presence both ancient and familiar. For millennia, humanity has turned its gaze upward, wondering at the unseen beings that dwell beyond the stars—the angels. Each culture, religion, and era has painted its own portrait of these messengers and guardians, granting them forms, functions, and realms. In essence, however, angels remain the mysterious bridge between the divine and mortal, embodying love, protection, and guidance.

In early human history, stories of angels often appeared as narratives of divine messengers bringing light to the chaos of earthly life. Across vast expanses of deserts and mountain ranges, people heard tales of luminous beings who appeared in dreams, rescued travelers, or shared knowledge from the heavens. The Egyptians called them "the Shining Ones," while the ancient Greeks spoke of them as intermediaries of the gods, draped in ethereal beauty. In each account, a shared thread persists: angels arrive not as rulers but as benevolent guides. They approach those in need and offer their wisdom, protection, or comfort without demanding worship or praise.

Their nature defies the limitations of human understanding, living both within the realm of light and in the shadows cast upon it. Angels are beings of celestial light, existing in dimensions where time and space as humans know them lose their hold. In their encounters with people, they often convey a deep sense of peace, sometimes felt as a gentle brush of presence, a whisper, or a sign in the language of dreams and intuition. It is said that, in these moments, we glimpse the vast networks of divine guidance that surround us.

At the heart of these beings' work is a simple yet profound purpose: to serve the divine will. For angels, "serving" is not an act of subjugation but one of love, a profound alignment with the currents of creation. Some angels carry out cosmic duties, presiding over vast expanses of the universe or guiding the movements of stars. Others work intimately with humanity, offering protection, inspiration, and healing. They are emissaries of divine wisdom, delivering messages from realms beyond and nudging the soul toward its purpose. Yet, in all of this, angels respect the sanctity of human free will. Though they watch closely, their intervention is delicate, awaiting the subtle call of an open heart or a sincere prayer.

Angels are also keepers of memory and prophecy. They are woven into the fabric of sacred texts, spanning the Hebrew Bible, the Quran, Christian scriptures, and beyond. In these ancient writings, they appear as harbingers of monumental change, their arrival often signifying moments of profound transformation. For some, they bring messages of hope and comfort, like Gabriel announcing to Mary the birth of a child, while for others, they act as protectors, like Michael, the archangel who is a warrior against dark forces. These stories, woven into human consciousness over centuries, have shaped the way we perceive angels—as messengers, warriors, guides, and companions who walk beside us on the paths we tread.

One of the most cherished roles assigned to angels is that of the guardian. Each person, according to ancient belief, is granted a personal guardian angel at birth, a celestial protector who remains by their side through life's journey. This belief crosses cultures and spiritual traditions, reflecting a universal hope that no one travels this world alone. It is said that these guardians intervene at times of great need, protecting from unseen dangers or offering quiet inspiration when choices are difficult. Some speak of close calls in which they felt inexplicably saved, others of subtle nudges that guided them through life's crossroads. And while many dismiss these moments as coincidence, those attuned to the presence of angels recognize them as divine intervention, a silent hand steering them toward safety and understanding.

Throughout history, stories of angelic intervention have been passed down, affirming the belief that these protectors do not simply observe—they act. Their language, however, is one of mystery, rich in symbols and omens. A sudden feeling of warmth, a flash of light, or a feather found in one's path are all signs that angels use to announce their nearness. In dreams, they may appear more clearly, revealing messages to those ready to listen. These signs, subtle yet unmistakable to those attuned to them, become an invitation to deepen our awareness of the spiritual world and our connection to it.

Thus, angels serve as both protectors and guides, honoring a sacred pact to aid humanity's journey back to the divine. In the labyrinth of life's trials, they remain constant, and in moments of profound sorrow or fear, their presence becomes an unspoken comfort. Some describe the feeling as a soft light or a gentle calm that washes over them. In these sacred moments, angels remind us of a truth often forgotten—that we are deeply loved and watched over by forces beyond our sight.

To approach the study of angels is to enter into a realm both sacred and infinite. It is to consider the possibility that we are not alone and that our lives are woven into a greater tapestry that stretches beyond mortal understanding. In glimpsing the role of angels, we begin to see how each of us is part of a larger cosmic story, written in the language of love, guidance, and divine protection. The purpose here is not to unravel every mystery but to kindle a reverent curiosity that honors the existence of these beings of light. They are, after all, part of a world that extends beyond the boundaries of human comprehension, a world that whispers to us in times of silence, beckoning us toward an ever-deeper connection with the divine.

In opening our hearts to the possibility of their presence, we begin a journey of spiritual understanding and gratitude. Each step, guided by their light, brings us closer to the recognition that angels are not mere myth but a living part of our world, offering their wisdom and guardianship as we move through life's mysteries.

Across countless traditions, the angelic hierarchy has captured the human imagination as an intricate order of beings, each serving a distinct purpose in the grand design of creation. To enter this hierarchy is to glimpse the organization of the spiritual world, where each angel, archangel, and celestial being contributes uniquely to the divine flow. This ancient order, mysterious and revered, is divided not by authority, but by function and mission, with each class of angel devoted to aspects of protection, guidance, knowledge, or healing.

Among the ranks of angels, some stand close to humanity, acting as guardians, while others inhabit realms far beyond, performing duties that sustain the harmony of the universe itself. At the foundation are the angels who attend directly to human life. These are the guardians and messengers, acting as a direct bridge between the celestial and earthly realms. They are said to travel freely between worlds, capable of assuming forms that allow them to interact with humans in subtle, gentle ways. Their purpose, always, is to uplift, protect, and guide, especially in moments of vulnerability, danger, or choice.

Above them lie the archangels, beings of immense light who embody specific qualities, like strength, healing, or wisdom. They are the ones whose names echo in sacred texts and rituals—Michael, the warrior; Gabriel, the herald; Raphael, the healer; and Uriel, the light-bearer. Each archangel radiates a powerful, almost magnetic energy that resonates with those who call upon them. Michael, with his sword of light, guards against darkness; Gabriel, with the clarity of his voice, delivers divine revelations; Raphael's gentle presence heals the wounded and the weary; while Uriel illuminates the shadows, revealing paths that may not have been visible. These archangels exist not only as individuals but as archetypes, each representing the purest form of divine virtues. When summoned, their presence is palpable, filling the air with a clarity and purpose that awakens the spirit.

Then, beyond these more familiar names, the hierarchy continues upward, each order progressively less concerned with earthly affairs and more with the maintenance of cosmic balance. The Cherubim, bearers of wisdom, and the Seraphim, beings of fiery devotion, exist in realms humans rarely perceive, engaged in the eternal adoration of the divine source. Through this structure, the spiritual world is meticulously maintained, with each order resonating at a specific frequency, contributing to a vast symphony of energy and intention. These angelic hierarchies are the invisible foundation upon which creation rests, working in unity to preserve the harmony of all existence.

The role of guardian angels, however, is unique within this grand structure. These beings of light dedicate themselves wholly to the well-being of their assigned human, weaving themselves into the very essence of the person's life. Unlike other angels, who may be called upon as needed, guardian angels are a constant presence. From the moment of birth, they accompany each soul, knowing the challenges and triumphs the journey will bring. Their intervention is quiet, often felt as a comforting sense of support in times of despair or a flash of inspiration in moments of confusion. They do not steer or command but offer guidance in subtle, non-intrusive ways, like a compass that gently nudges rather than dictates.

Guardian angels can be invoked consciously or simply acknowledged with heartfelt intent. In times of need, when the heart reaches out for solace, these angels respond, often with a calm reassurance that lifts the spirit. Signs of their presence vary, manifesting uniquely for each person. Some feel a cool breeze in a closed room, a sudden sensation of peace, or perhaps find white feathers in unexpected places. Others report sensing their guardian's presence through dreams, where their angel appears to guide or comfort them in symbolic or direct ways. Regardless of the form it takes, a guardian angel's presence is unmistakable, drawing one closer to a sense of purpose, protection, and spiritual companionship.

The angels' ability to intervene in daily life depends on free will. Rarely will they override a person's choices, but they will do all they can to offer protection when called upon. In moments of crisis, an angel's guidance may come as a flash of insight, an unanticipated change in circumstance, or a voice from within that feels like intuition but carries a clarity and urgency beyond ordinary instinct. The purpose here is not to alter life's course entirely but to keep one aligned with the path that best honors their higher purpose.

Many ancient teachings explain that guardian angels also serve as silent record-keepers, attuned to each soul's growth, challenges, and milestones. They understand the spiritual significance of each experience and offer encouragement to help individuals see the lessons inherent in their journey. Some say that when life's end approaches, it is the guardian angel who accompanies the soul on its journey beyond, acting as a gentle guide through the transition, ensuring that no one is ever truly alone.

It is no surprise, then, that in moments of great need or confusion, guardian angels are often the first to answer a heartfelt prayer. Through them, divine love finds an accessible and immediate expression. The guardians feel no judgment, only a compassionate awareness of the human experience. They act with the patience of one who sees life from an eternal perspective, never perturbed by setbacks or challenges. Their only desire is to help each soul navigate life's complexities, striving toward inner peace and purpose.

For those who wish to deepen this connection, guardian angels can be invited into daily life through simple acts of reverence and trust. A morning moment of silence, a whispered request for guidance, or even an expression of gratitude can strengthen the bond, creating a foundation of mutual respect and love. In times of meditation or reflection, one may even sense their guardian's energy as a calm, benevolent presence just beyond the veil of ordinary awareness. This connection, though unseen, becomes one of the most profound relationships in a person's life, a source of comfort and guidance that persists through all circumstances.

As we move closer to understanding this hierarchy, the relationship between humanity and the angelic world unfolds like a divine partnership. Guardian angels are at the heart of this union, embodying a love that transcends words, a presence that is patient and eternal. Through the gentle guidance of these celestial beings, we are reminded that each life is cherished and watched over, and in return, we may honor their presence with trust and openness, allowing their light to guide us along the path of our own becoming.

Chapter 2
Guardian Angels

The presence of a guardian angel is subtle yet constant, felt not with the senses but within the heart. Though they remain invisible to the eye, guardian angels dwell closer to each person than their own breath, woven into the fabric of existence. They are companions, protectors, and silent observers who intervene at the most pivotal moments, waiting for the right instant to guide with a gentle whisper or a moment of clarity. Many speak of feeling watched over, held safely even in the most precarious situations, as though an unseen hand lifts them from danger's edge. In the silent company of a guardian angel, life itself takes on a gentler tone, as if something powerful and compassionate forever watches from beyond.

Guardian angels are attuned to the deepest needs of those they protect. They perceive emotions, thoughts, and intentions, but with a compassion unmarred by judgment. Their care is timeless, beyond the fleeting nature of human feelings. It is said that, even before birth, a guardian angel is assigned to each soul, their only purpose being to offer guidance and companionship through life's journey. This profound responsibility is undertaken with a purity of intent, a love so deep that it transcends human understanding, reaching into the soul's essence.

In countless traditions and folklore, stories of these protectors emerge as sacred narratives of faith and mystery. They are often portrayed as wise yet gentle presences, capable of great power and tender compassion. In certain cultures, guardian angels are depicted as figures of light or with gentle, watchful eyes that see beyond the veil of earthly life. While some tales recount miraculous escapes from harm attributed to their intervention, others speak of subtler guidance—a dream, a symbol, or even a small gesture that nudges the heart toward a path of truth or safety. These stories remind us that angels do not control but instead offer us a compass by which we may find our way.

Encounters with guardian angels vary as widely as the human souls they protect. Some feel their presence as a warmth that spreads through the chest in moments of sorrow, as though a caring hand rests upon the heart. Others sense them as a calm voice in the mind, guiding away from danger or gently redirecting them when they veer from their path. Those who keep a keen eye for signs may find feathers in unexpected places or notice a sudden flash of light at the edge of vision—subtle but unmistakable signs of a guardian's quiet presence.

Despite their commitment to the souls they protect, guardian angels respect human freedom and do not interfere in every matter. They are bound by the sacred law of free will, stepping in only when intervention aligns with the highest good or when their guidance is sought openly. However, they are watchful, attentive, always prepared to act should a moment of crisis or vulnerability arise. When called upon through heartfelt prayer or intention, guardian angels respond immediately, bringing a sense of protection or a feeling of clarity to the seeker. Many who seek answers in times of confusion or despair report feeling a wave of calm, a certain knowingness that arises from nowhere and leaves no doubt of its source.

In times of great peril, the intervention of a guardian angel may feel almost miraculous. Countless stories tell of last-minute rescues and inexplicable events where people narrowly escape harm. A driver stops abruptly just before a sudden accident, a child finds a way home through unfamiliar streets, a traveler misses a doomed flight. Skeptics may call these coincidences, but those who have felt their guardian angel's touch know there is something beyond the veil, something that intervenes with perfect timing. To believers, such moments are the undeniable work of a guardian angel, offering protection with a precision that defies logic.

Guardian angels, however, also protect in the quiet, unseen ways that shape a life toward its higher potential. They bring comfort in sorrow, offering silent encouragement when courage wanes. In moments of joy, they share in the lightness of the heart, rejoicing in the fulfillment of life's purpose. When life's challenges mount, guardian angels shield the spirit from despair, offering strength to persist. They are steadfast companions in every trial, a source of peace through all turmoil.

The bond between a person and their guardian angel strengthens with awareness and openness. Though their presence is eternal, an invitation to connect allows them to work more directly. This can be done through simple words, a moment of reflection, or silent acknowledgment. Those who establish regular connection practices find the sense of their guardian angel's presence deepens over time. Meditations, prayers, or even a heartfelt expression of gratitude creates a bridge, a kind of invitation for closer communion. Through such practices, the veil between realms grows thinner, allowing for a clearer exchange of guidance and support.

In the quiet spaces of the mind, guardian angels may communicate, offering insights or a sudden surge of intuition. Some find their guardian angel speaks in dreams, appearing in symbolic or familiar forms that carry a message meant to guide or reassure. Others feel a distinct sensation—a gentle weight on the shoulder, a warm rush of calm—that arrives in moments of worry or indecision. In these instances, the angel's message is simple but profound: you are not alone.

Guardian angels work patiently and diligently, never imposing their will but always offering their wisdom. They remain with each person through life's trials, growth, and transformation, even beyond death's threshold. When the time of transition arrives, it is often believed that the guardian angel is the one who gently guides the soul, helping it cross into realms beyond. In this sacred moment, their presence is a comfort, a reminder of love that neither time nor death can separate.

For those who wish to cultivate a deeper bond, practices such as lighting a candle, saying a prayer, or carrying a small token as a reminder of their guardian's presence are simple but powerful acts. Acknowledging one's guardian angel creates a sacred space within, a place of calm that invites the angelic presence to reside more openly in daily life. This awareness opens a channel, creating a silent understanding between human and guardian that fosters trust and closeness.

Ultimately, guardian angels are as much a part of us as our breath, guiding each of us toward the fulfillment of our higher purpose. They do not seek recognition or reverence but rather a willing heart and an open mind. When invited, they bring a lightness and protection that infuse every aspect of life, nurturing the soul with love that surpasses the bounds of time. Through them, we come to understand that even in the darkest moments, we are cherished, watched over, and guided by a force that sees not just the person we are, but the divine being we are becoming.

The presence of a guardian angel is a thread, delicate but unbreakable, that binds each of us to the divine. Yet for many, the question arises: how can one perceive and recognize these angelic companions in daily life? This connection, while subtle, can be strengthened through practice, intuition, and trust. Guardian angels, though unseen, communicate in ways that transcend ordinary perception, weaving their presence through moments of stillness, symbols, and the quiet wisdom that emerges within us.

One of the most profound ways to recognize a guardian angel is by learning to interpret signs, those subtle hints that nudge the heart. Many who feel their angel's presence report a recurring feeling of warmth, a gentle touch, or even a rush of peace that washes over them unexpectedly. Feathers, for example, are widely regarded as symbols of angelic presence, appearing in the most unlikely places, as if to say, *"I am here."* For some, it is the sudden appearance of a particular number sequence, like 111 or 444, resonating with an intuitive message. These symbols, though small, are like whispered reassurances that the path is being watched over.

In addition to physical signs, guardian angels often communicate through the language of emotions. It is not uncommon to feel a spontaneous sense of calm, love, or clarity when an angel is near. In moments of confusion, a gentle wave of reassurance may come as if from nowhere, offering a sense of direction or perspective. Those who tune into this subtle emotional guidance often find that it steers them through life's challenges with a sense of grace. By practicing mindfulness, becoming aware of shifts in one's emotional state, a person can begin to recognize when their guardian is reaching out, providing a shield of calm or a nudge toward wise choices.

A profound aspect of strengthening the bond with a guardian angel is through dreams. When the conscious mind rests, the barriers between the earthly and spiritual realms grow thin, making it easier for angelic messages to come through. In dreams, guardian angels may appear in familiar or symbolic forms, offering guidance or messages in ways that are deeply personal. To attune oneself to such dreams, a simple ritual before bed can serve as an invitation—lighting a candle, saying a short prayer, or even setting an intention to remember any message that may come. Upon waking, writing down even the smallest fragments of dreams can reveal patterns or themes that, over time, uncover a thread of guidance or reassurance.

Another way to deepen the connection with one's guardian angel is through meditation. This sacred practice allows for quietness within, opening a door through which the angel's energy can be felt more clearly. In a quiet space, with distractions set aside, visualizing a gentle light surrounding the body helps invite the angel's presence. Some find that a specific color, such as gold or white, helps to evoke the feeling of angelic closeness. By focusing on the breath and letting thoughts drift by like clouds, the mind clears, creating a serene atmosphere where the guardian angel's voice—a quiet intuition, an image, a feeling of warmth—can be perceived. With practice, this state of peace becomes familiar, and the presence of the angel becomes as natural as the rhythm of breath.

Certain prayers and affirmations also serve as tools to strengthen the bond with a guardian angel. Words spoken with sincerity carry an energy that transcends language, creating a bridge between realms. A simple invocation such as, *"Guardian angel, please guide and protect me,"* resonates deeply. These words, repeated with intention, remind both the angel and the one calling of their shared purpose. With practice, these prayers act as a powerful centering tool, drawing the angel closer and fortifying the individual's sense of safety and inner peace.

As the connection deepens, signs of the guardian angel's presence often become clearer, appearing in moments of both stillness and need. For those who seek an even closer relationship, gratitude is a powerful and transformative act. Taking a moment each day to acknowledge the angel's presence and offer thanks, even in simple words, opens the heart. This gratitude creates an energy that resonates throughout the soul, reinforcing the relationship with the angel in ways that cannot be measured. In this practice of acknowledging and giving thanks, an individual learns to feel their guardian's presence as a constant, guiding force, recognizing the signs of their angel as something precious and enduring.

With time, those who pursue a close bond with their guardian angel often develop an intuitive understanding of the messages offered to them. Small decisions, once burdensome, become clearer as guidance flows with ease. The gentle nudges and feelings of protection come to be recognized as aspects of the guardian angel's work, illuminating even the smallest choices. Those who open themselves to this connection feel the comforting presence of a guardian not only in moments of need but in the everyday rhythm of life, where the angel's influence adds a sense of peace, resilience, and clarity.

In times of adversity, this relationship offers a form of protection that surpasses any physical shield. Through their guardian angel, a person can find strength to navigate life's storms with an unshakable sense of hope and resilience. These beings act not as shields against pain but as allies in overcoming it, offering wisdom and love that support the soul's growth. Many have experienced a sudden clarity, a newfound strength, or an inner voice that urges them to keep going in their darkest hours. This is the guardian angel's influence—supporting, empowering, and guiding from a place of unconditional love.

For those who have walked alongside their guardian angel in life's journey, the bond becomes like that of an old, trusted friend. No ritual or prayer is necessary; a simple thought, a quiet reaching out, is enough. Over time, guardian angels reveal themselves not only as protectors but as reminders of the soul's own light and capacity for love. Through this relationship, individuals come to understand that while the angels protect, it is ultimately the human heart, open and receptive, that allows their presence to shine fully.

The relationship with a guardian angel is unique, a personal and sacred bond that exists not out of obligation, but out of love. To accept the presence of a guardian angel is to embrace the quiet mystery of life, to acknowledge that each person's journey is cherished, watched over, and blessed in ways that may never fully be understood. In moments of stillness, when the heart listens, guardian angels draw close, offering their guidance and love, a light that forever accompanies the soul. Through this bond, we come to recognize that our journeys are shared, guided by hands unseen, hearts intertwined, and voices that, while silent, echo within us eternally.

Chapter 3
Preparing for the Ritual

To prepare for communion with the angelic realm, one must begin by creating a space that resonates with clarity and peace—a sacred environment where the physical meets the spiritual. The creation of such a space is an art, a practice that allows the practitioner to enter a state of openness and reverence. When set with intention, this environment becomes more than mere surroundings; it transforms into a portal, a place where angels and humans may meet, where divine light and earthly presence intersect. Each object, each scent, and each sound is chosen to guide the spirit toward that mysterious connection, where words fall away, and only presence remains.

The first steps involve a deliberate clearing of the area. Physical cleanliness holds symbolic power; dust and clutter are more than material distractions, for they can obstruct energy and diminish the room's capacity to hold sacred intention. With each piece of furniture carefully arranged, each surface wiped free of dust, and every corner given attention, the practitioner is in essence carving out a space that honors the presence of angels, inviting them with respect and intention. In this setting, simplicity is a virtue. An uncluttered space speaks of openness, a readiness to receive guidance without expectation or interference.

After the space is physically cleansed, the next layer of preparation involves harmonizing the energy of the environment. Natural elements—earth, fire, water, and air—are invited into the room to reflect the balance of nature itself. A small bowl of pure water can represent emotional clarity, while a crystal or stone symbolizes grounding, connecting the practitioner to the steady strength of the earth. Each element, whether a flame flickering on a candle or the cool touch of water, resonates with its unique energy, awakening aspects of spirit that align the practitioner with angelic frequencies.

Candles are perhaps the most potent tools in creating this sacred space, as their light mirrors the very essence of angels—pure, guiding, gentle. A white candle, symbolizing purity and peace, serves as a beacon, illuminating the path for angelic presence. Its flame, though small, transforms the room, casting a warm glow that invites introspection and calm. Lighting a candle is a ritual in itself, a gesture that marks the beginning of sacred time and signifies the opening of the heart to angelic presence. For those who wish to deepen the practice, adding colored candles can align with specific intentions. Blue, for instance, resonates with healing and communication, while gold symbolizes wisdom and divine illumination. Each color becomes a language, a vibration that communicates the practitioner's intent to the angelic realm.

Incense and aromatic herbs carry their own language, whispering to the senses and lifting the spirit. Sage, cedar, or palo santo can be burned to purify the space, their smoke acting as a cleansing veil that clears lingering energies and leaves the room ripe for communion. Lavender, gentle and calming, or frankincense, deeply grounding and mysterious, fills the space with an atmosphere that elevates the senses and prepares the mind to receive. This layer of scent transcends simple fragrance; it acts on the soul, awakening memory, opening perception, and allowing the space to resonate with frequencies that reach beyond the physical. In this way, incense becomes more than an aroma; it is a guide, gently escorting the spirit toward clarity and communion.

Objects chosen for a sacred space are never random; each one holds meaning, carrying the intention of the practitioner and reflecting their sincerity. Crystals, for instance, amplify energy, their natural structures reflecting and intensifying the purity of the practitioner's focus. Clear quartz, known as a "master healer," resonates at a high frequency, purifying the energy around it and enhancing spiritual communication. Celestite, a crystal often associated with angelic realms, radiates a calming, peaceful energy, inviting a sense of closeness to divine beings. The careful placement of these stones is an art, a silent language that speaks of the desire to create a bridge between realms.

A small offering or token—a feather, a flower, or a handwritten note—can serve as an emblem of intention, an acknowledgment of gratitude toward the angelic beings who may visit. Such gestures, humble yet sincere, are symbols of respect and openness, reflecting the heart's readiness to receive and to honor the unseen. In the process of preparing a sacred space, the practitioner is not simply arranging objects but is creating a relationship, a dance of energies that invites the angels to draw near.

The room's energy is further influenced by sound, whether in the form of soft music, chimes, or silence itself. Gentle sounds act as a balm, soothing any restlessness and aligning the practitioner's vibration with that of the spiritual world. A quiet bell or the resonant tone of a singing bowl can break the silence with intention, marking moments of transition and preparing the heart for angelic connection. If silence is chosen, it should be deep and undisturbed, an open canvas upon which the practitioner's thoughts and feelings can settle. In this quietness, the subtle language of angels—the whispers, impressions, and intuitions—can be felt most profoundly.

Once the environment is prepared, there is one final step: entering the sacred space with a mind cleared of distractions and a heart centered in humility and openness. A simple grounding exercise, such as mindful breathing or a short meditation, roots the practitioner firmly in the present, aligning their awareness with the purity of the prepared space. With each breath, tension is released, and thoughts are softened, creating an internal stillness that matches the external harmony. This state of presence, free of expectation and filled with quiet wonder, is the most profound invitation one can extend to an angelic presence.

In these final moments of preparation, an intention is set—simple, sincere, and focused. Whether one seeks guidance, protection, or merely the gentle touch of angelic companionship, this intention is held gently in the heart. No elaborate words are needed; the language of intention is felt, resonating quietly yet powerfully. With this readiness, the practitioner becomes a living part of the sacred space, aligned and attuned, waiting with reverence.

The sacred space is now prepared, not merely as a physical area, but as a threshold where dimensions touch and energies flow freely. It is a space filled with intention, a reflection of the practitioner's soul. As one stands within this place, feeling the subtle energy that has been created, there is a sense of anticipation, a feeling that something unseen draws near. In this space, the heart is quieted, the mind is calm, and the soul waits, poised to enter into a silent conversation with the angelic realm, where words are unnecessary, and only light remains.

To deepen the sacred space, each object, each gesture, and every intention is elevated, resonating with a purpose that transcends ordinary preparation. This process is not merely an act of setting a stage but of entering a realm where every element harmonizes with the angelic presence. As the practitioner refines this environment, the space itself becomes a living channel, ready to receive energies that exist beyond the limits of perception.

Consecrating objects within the sacred space is a gesture of dedication and respect, infusing them with purpose. Each item—whether a candle, a crystal, or a symbol—holds its own essence, but through consecration, these objects resonate with the practitioner's energy, amplifying the connection to the angelic realm. This consecration can be as simple or as elaborate as the heart desires. A few quiet words of blessing, a silent intention, or the subtle touch of breath over each object is enough to infuse it with life. Through this act, the items chosen for the sacred space become allies in the journey, conduits for angelic energy that amplify the intentions held within the practitioner's heart.

Crystals, known for their capacity to store and radiate energy, benefit greatly from consecration. To consecrate a crystal, one may hold it to the heart, closing the eyes and breathing deeply. The crystal's energy, steady and strong, merges with the practitioner's intention as they silently ask the crystal to serve as a beacon for angelic guidance and protection. With this act, the crystal is no longer just a stone; it becomes a partner in the spiritual endeavor, radiating its subtle light and forming a bridge to realms unseen. As each crystal is placed within the space, it forms a web of energy that strengthens the presence of angels, guiding the practitioner into deeper alignment.

The act of preparing sacred symbols also carries profound significance. Symbols, ancient in their essence, hold the power to focus and direct energy. Simple symbols, such as an angelic cross or circles drawn in the air, invite harmony into the space. For those inclined, sacred geometry, such as the Flower of Life or the Star of David, can be drawn or placed in the room. These geometric shapes are not mere patterns; they are energetic maps that align with universal order, bringing harmony to the environment and invoking a sense of sacred order. The practitioner may trace these symbols in the air or visualize them hovering softly above the altar or center of the room, each one a silent invitation for angelic beings to draw closer.

Incorporating specific natural elements within the space also enhances spiritual receptivity. By using herbs and resins known for their cleansing and protective properties, the practitioner adds a layer of grounding and purity. Sage, cedar, or rosemary, when burned, releases a smoke that not only purifies but sanctifies. These herbs are ancient allies, used throughout history to bridge the worlds of spirit and matter. Their presence within the sacred space offers an invitation for angels to descend, guiding the practitioner into a closer relationship with the divine. Placing a small bowl of salt or earth in the space grounds the energy, anchoring angelic presence in the here and now, stabilizing the flow of spirit within the confines of the earthly realm.

Another vital aspect of sacred space preparation is setting the atmosphere with light. Candles provide more than illumination; their flames act as symbols of the soul's desire to connect, to shine, to transcend. Lighting each candle with intention, one may visualize the flame as a pathway that angels travel, drawn to the purity and simplicity of light. A blue or violet candle, for example, resonates with angelic frequencies, inviting peace and higher understanding. Watching the flame, steady and unwavering, brings the mind into stillness, allowing thoughts to settle and emotions to quiet, creating an inner space as clear as the physical one prepared.

The process of aligning the energy within the space continues with sound. Bells, chimes, or singing bowls create vibrations that purify, inviting clarity. The resonance of a single bell, struck softly, seems to linger in the air, weaving into the environment a sense of calm that extends into the soul. For those who prefer silence, this too holds power; a complete stillness allows the subtlest of energies to be felt, unbroken and pure. In the silence, the veil between worlds grows thin, enabling angelic energy to enter unencumbered. Whether through sound or silence, the atmosphere shifts from ordinary to extraordinary, a place where energies flow freely, unhindered by the distractions of the outer world.

Once all is in place, the practitioner may take a final moment to stand within the space, feeling its energy. A brief pause, a quiet breath, allows them to tune into the presence that now fills the room. The energy will feel distinct—clear, calm, and expansive, like stepping into a quiet forest or a sacred hall. This is not merely a room; it is now a consecrated threshold, a realm where spiritual connections are nurtured, where communication flows easily. Here, surrounded by objects of intention and immersed in the calm of the space, the practitioner becomes both witness and participant in an unfolding mystery.

One of the most profound gestures of preparation is to attune personal energy to the space itself. A simple ritual of mindful breathing aligns the body and mind, allowing the practitioner to harmonize with the energy they have cultivated. With each inhalation, they draw in peace and clarity, and with each exhalation, they release tension and distractions. This breathing connects the inner self to the sacred space, creating a unified field of calm and openness. In this state, the heart opens, the mind quiets, and the spirit aligns with the angelic presence, ready to receive.

For those who wish to express gratitude, a short prayer of thanks can be offered before beginning. Gratitude, as the language of the heart, invites angels to remain close, resonating with their energy of love and light. A simple statement of thanks to the divine, to the angels, or to the sacred space itself is enough. This gratitude need not be elaborate; it is the sincerity of the gesture that resonates, reverberating through the room and filling the air with a quiet joy. Through this act, the practitioner acknowledges the presence of unseen forces, welcoming them not as strangers but as beloved companions.

The sacred space is now ready, transformed into a vessel of light and intention. Each element—light, sound, scent, and symbol—holds a piece of the practitioner's purpose, woven together into a fabric that connects them with the angelic realm. In this place of calm, where distractions are absent and peace reigns, the air feels charged, vibrant, as though alive with possibilities. It is here, in this space lovingly prepared, that angels are welcomed, where their presence becomes as tangible as breath, as real as the warmth of the candle's glow.

In entering this space, the practitioner steps across a threshold, leaving behind the noise of the outer world and entering a realm of pure connection. They stand poised, ready to listen, to feel, to open themselves to the wisdom and guidance that angels offer. And in this moment, all that is required is a heart attuned to the quiet, a soul ready to receive, and a space that invites the angels to draw near, surrounding the practitioner in light and grace.

Chapter 4
Energy Cleansing

The first step to inviting angelic energies into one's life is to purify the body and environment, transforming them into vessels of light and openness. Energy cleansing holds ancient roots, practiced across civilizations to prepare the soul and space for connection with higher realms. This process is not a mere ritual but an alchemical preparation—a purification that allows the practitioner to rise into a state of heightened receptivity, attuned to the sacred frequencies angels carry. In shedding the residues of daily concerns, worries, and attachments, the spirit becomes an open vessel ready to receive the pure presence of angelic beings.

Cleansing begins with the environment. Space carries energies, absorbing vibrations from people, experiences, and even thoughts. Thus, a room becomes a sanctuary when its energy is clarified and elevated. Simple tools—smoke from sacred herbs, crystals, or salt water—serve to purify the space of lingering energies, creating an atmosphere that feels calm and radiant. Burning sage, for instance, is a traditional method to cleanse and elevate energy, the smoke drifting through every corner, reaching hidden spaces, and releasing stagnant energy back to the earth. Cedar and rosemary serve similarly, each herb bringing a unique energetic quality that infuses the room with peace and calm. The aroma rises, carrying with it any residue of doubt, fatigue, or distress, leaving the space open, fresh, and ready for angelic presence.

After the physical space is purified, the practitioner turns to their own energy. The body, like the space it inhabits, holds and absorbs energies from daily interactions and thoughts. When preparing for angelic communion, it is essential to shed these layers of energetic residue, returning to a state of clarity and peace. One of the most effective methods for personal cleansing is the ritual of a spiritual bath. Using specific herbs, salts, or essential oils, the practitioner steps into the water, visualizing every drop washing away stress, fear, and attachments. Rosemary for protection, lavender for calm, and basil for purification are commonly used to transform the water into a balm that refreshes the spirit. As the water embraces the body, the spirit is soothed, cleansed, and freed from the weight of worldly concerns, inviting a lightness that mirrors the presence of angels.

Crystals, too, offer powerful support in this cleansing. Amethyst, for instance, radiates a gentle yet potent energy that clears negativity and aligns the spirit with higher realms. To use crystals in cleansing, one might simply hold a stone to the heart, breathing deeply, allowing its energy to resonate through the body. Clear quartz amplifies this effect, drawing out impurities from the aura and fortifying it with a pure, high vibration. In the embrace of these stones, the practitioner's energy field becomes balanced, prepared to resonate with the angelic frequencies they seek.

Mindful breathing serves as another vital tool, simple yet transformative. Each inhalation brings in light and peace, while each exhalation releases tension and distraction. By focusing intently on the breath, the practitioner roots themselves in the present, where angelic presence is most perceptible. Breathing deeply, visualizing light filling the body, each breath cleanses and opens, allowing the spirit to ascend toward a state of readiness. This rhythmic breath aligns the mind and body, creating a conduit through which angels may enter, their presence sensed within the stillness that breathing creates.

As these cleansing practices unfold, an energy shift occurs, subtle but profound. The practitioner feels lighter, sensations more attuned, emotions steadier. The physical world grows quiet, and the inner realm opens, creating a space of purity, a vessel ready to receive angelic guidance. In this state, distractions fall away; the heart grows calm, and the mind, no longer tangled in daily concerns, becomes a clear mirror for divine reflection.

Once the body and space are purified, a final gesture is to seal this cleansing with an intention—a statement of purpose that guides and holds the practitioner's focus. This intention can be a simple phrase, such as, *"I cleanse this space and myself to welcome angelic light,"* or *"I prepare myself as a channel for divine presence."* Through this intention, the act of cleansing transcends ritual, becoming a conscious alignment with the energies one hopes to invite. This intention seals the cleansing, infusing it with purpose and directing the energy toward the highest outcome.

To maintain this purity, the practitioner may consider incorporating cleansing as a regular practice, a grounding ritual that centers and aligns. Whether through daily mindful breathing, weekly cleansing with sage, or periodic spiritual baths, these practices ensure that the connection with angelic beings remains strong, the vessel of the self kept clear, light, and receptive. In the continuity of cleansing, the spirit remains ever attuned to the presence of angels, ready to receive guidance and grace.

With space purified and the self aligned, a door opens between realms, and the practitioner finds themselves in a place of tranquility, embraced by a sense of warmth and calm. Here, the presence of angels is near, sensed not in grand visions but in the delicate shifts within—small moments of peace, a softening of thoughts, a deep and abiding sense of love. In this purity, the practitioner's energy aligns effortlessly with the angelic, becoming a channel through which the presence, wisdom, and protection of angels flow freely.

For those seeking to deepen their connection with the angelic realm, energy cleansing is not merely preparation but a way of life, an ongoing practice that refines sensitivity and enhances spiritual receptivity. As the practitioner advances, cleansing becomes a more nuanced and personal ritual, moving beyond the physical to reach deeper layers of spirit and intention. Through advanced practices, the soul becomes attuned to subtle energies, moving freely between states of calm and openness where angelic presence is felt with clarity and ease.

One of the most potent methods for deep cleansing is through the repetition of mantras, phrases of power that elevate energy and dissolve blockages. Specific mantras, chosen with care, resonate deeply, creating sound vibrations that cleanse the mind and spirit. A mantra can be as simple as the word *"light"* or a phrase such as *"I release all that no longer serves me."* With each repetition, these words flow through the practitioner's energy field, breaking through energetic stagnation and releasing layers of tension and doubt. This rhythm, steady and continuous, lifts the spirit, aligning it with the realm of angels. By speaking or whispering these words, the practitioner moves closer to the purity that angels embody, their voice becoming an echo of the divine call they wish to receive.

Affirmations complement this practice, serving as seeds of intention planted within the mind and heart. Simple yet powerful phrases, such as *"I am open to divine guidance,"* create an energetic resonance that aligns the practitioner with angelic frequencies. Each affirmation, spoken with sincerity, dissolves mental barriers and allows angelic light to flow freely. In the quiet repetition of these affirmations, a clearing occurs, a soft yet steady movement that carries away distractions, fears, and uncertainties. Through this process, the practitioner becomes an open channel, cleansed of inner noise, resonating clearly with the realm they seek.

Physical techniques are also essential in deepening energy cleansing. The body, as a vessel of spirit, benefits greatly from practices that align it with higher energies. Herbal baths, taken with specific plants or oils, provide a tangible sense of purification. Herbs such as mint, rosemary, and eucalyptus, when steeped in water, create a bath that cleanses both body and aura, their energies dissolving residual negativity and inviting clarity. Stepping into this water becomes an act of renewal, each herb chosen with care to support the practitioner's intention. With each drop, the mind and body release old energies, and the aura, refreshed, reflects a state of openness and readiness.

Incorporating breathing exercises is another powerful technique, transforming breath into a tool of healing and realignment. Practicing a steady, rhythmic breath, inhaling deeply and exhaling fully, releases stagnant energy and sharpens the spirit's sensitivity. One can visualize each inhale as drawing in light, while each exhale releases dark clouds or tensions that have gathered. With each breath, the practitioner descends deeper into a state of stillness, where the whispers of angels may be perceived. This breathing practice, gentle yet profound, purifies the energy body, attuning it to the presence of angels, whose own energy is as pure and expansive as light.

Advanced visualization techniques serve as a bridge between the mind's inner eye and the energies that surround it. Visualizing oneself bathed in white light or within a sphere of golden energy creates a shield of purity. This sphere not only protects but also refines the practitioner's aura, lifting it into alignment with angelic vibrations. Each visualization, held steadily within the mind, strengthens the connection, illuminating the path for angels to draw near. This practice becomes a space of refuge, a moment of communion, where the mind quiets, and the spirit brightens.

Another transformative practice is the use of sound, either through chanting, singing bowls, or even humming. Sound, with its ability to penetrate layers of the self, reaches the energetic field, vibrating through tension, cleansing, and clearing. Singing bowls, for instance, emit tones that purify, each vibration rippling through the aura, dissolving any disharmony. With each note, the practitioner feels their energy realign, as though each sound has brushed away residue, leaving behind only clarity and openness. Through these resonant tones, the veil between realms becomes lighter, thinner, and the presence of angels is felt as a gentle pressure in the air, a sense of warmth that draws near.

In moments of great need or deeper clearing, invoking a specific angel, such as Archangel Michael, is a powerful practice. Michael, often called upon for protection and purification, is associated with a sword of light that cuts through dense energies and dissolves obstacles. A simple invocation, such as, *"Archangel Michael, I call upon you for protection and cleansing,"* can create an immediate sense of peace and safety. Imagining his presence, a beam of light descending and enveloping the practitioner, instills courage and fortifies the spirit. In this light, any negativity dissolves, leaving the practitioner aligned, uplifted, and fully open to angelic guidance.

To conclude these practices, one may ground their energy, sealing in the purity achieved. Grounding involves reconnecting with the earth's steady energy, anchoring the spirit back into the present. A moment of standing barefoot on the ground, placing a hand on the heart, or holding a grounding crystal such as hematite or black tourmaline brings stability. Through this act, the practitioner's energy, refined and open, is drawn back into the body, anchored and steady. This grounding creates a balance, allowing the high vibrations of angelic energy to integrate gently with the earthly self.

As these practices grow familiar, they form a daily rhythm, a foundation that keeps the practitioner's energy clear and open, ever attuned to the presence of angels. In moments of doubt, or when the spirit feels heavy, these practices serve as a return to center, a reminder of the light that always surrounds and supports. Through cleansing, the practitioner not only prepares for rituals but cultivates a space within, a heart open and ready to meet angelic presence at any moment.

Thus, through layers of purification, the spirit shines, becoming a vessel of light and receptivity. Angels, drawn to this purity, draw near, not as distant beings but as close companions, their presence felt in every breath, every quiet moment of peace. In this state of openness, the practitioner finds that angelic guidance flows naturally, an intuitive knowing, a quiet assurance that the spirit is connected, cherished, and surrounded by light. The cleansing is complete, the spirit attuned, and the path open, inviting the presence and wisdom of angels into every facet of life.

Chapter 5
Intention in Ritual

Intention lies at the heart of every ritual, shaping it from within, directing its energy toward the realm of angels with clarity and purpose. Before calling upon these beings, the practitioner must first define a clear, sincere intention, for this focus acts as a beacon, guiding angelic presence to the one who calls. Intention is not merely a mental act; it is a conscious alignment of heart, mind, and soul, a declaration that opens a pathway between worlds. It is through intention that the practitioner's desires, hopes, and needs are transformed into pure energy, reaching beyond the veil and inviting the assistance and guidance of angels.

To begin, the practitioner quiets the mind, allowing thoughts to settle like still water, creating space for a focused intention to arise. This clarity forms the foundation upon which all angelic rituals rest. A moment of silent reflection allows the true need of the heart to emerge, unburdened by distractions or fleeting desires. In this silence, one must ask, *"What do I truly seek?"* This question holds power, for it directs attention inward, to the essence of what the soul longs for. Whether seeking protection, guidance, healing, or simply companionship, this inner clarity sharpens the intention, making it a thread of light that angels may follow.

As the intention takes shape, it is important that it be simple yet sincere. Angels, attuned to the energies of love and truth, respond most clearly to intentions formed from the heart. Rather than complex or lengthy requests, a pure intention that resonates with one's core is more effective. Phrases such as, *"I seek guidance in my path forward,"* or, *"I ask for protection and peace,"* resonate deeply, carrying the weight of sincerity and focus. When spoken, these words vibrate with clarity, aligning the practitioner with angelic presence. Through simplicity, the practitioner's intention becomes a clear note, a sound that rises easily, unencumbered by layers of doubt or distraction.

To deepen this alignment, the practitioner must also ensure that their emotional state resonates with the intention they set. Emotions are powerful guides, and to reach the angelic realm, the practitioner must approach with a heart free from fear, doubt, or resentment. A state of peace, gratitude, or love enhances the intention, refining its purity and power. Should the heart feel unsettled, it is beneficial to take a few moments to breathe deeply, releasing any lingering emotions that may cloud the intention. In this state of emotional harmony, the practitioner's request becomes a channel of light, a direct line that angels can recognize and respond to, as it mirrors the peaceful and loving nature of their own realm.

Visualization can further strengthen the focus of intention, creating a mental image that represents the request. The mind, when harnessed through visualization, becomes a powerful ally, enhancing the resonance of the intention. The practitioner may visualize a soft, radiant light around them, representing angelic presence, or imagine a scene that embodies the fulfillment of their request. For example, if seeking protection, one might visualize themselves surrounded by a shield of light, impenetrable and glowing. This mental image sharpens the intention, transforming it into something tangible, a vision that angels may perceive as an invitation to draw near.

Writing the intention also solidifies it, transforming abstract thought into something concrete. Placing the intention on paper, in clear, direct language, strengthens the practitioner's focus. Writing is itself an act of commitment, a ritual that captures the essence of the desire and holds it in the physical realm. By creating this physical representation, the practitioner establishes a point of connection, a reminder of the intention's presence. After writing, the practitioner may place the paper on an altar, under a candle, or carry it with them as a token, a tangible representation of the energy they wish to send forth.

Each ritual carries a unique purpose, and as such, the intention must be set anew with each practice. This is not a mere repetition, but an opportunity to refine and deepen one's focus. With each setting of intention, the practitioner's energy sharpens, growing familiar with the subtle rhythms and tones of the angelic realm. Through this practice, setting intention becomes second nature, an intuitive preparation that centers and attunes the practitioner, allowing for a seamless flow between desire and divine response.

In these quiet moments before the ritual begins, gratitude becomes an essential part of setting intention. Expressing gratitude for the guidance that is yet to come opens the heart further, creating an atmosphere of trust and receptivity. This gratitude, sincere and unhurried, need not be elaborate—simple words or a moment of silent appreciation suffice. It is through gratitude that the practitioner aligns with the angels' essence, creating a vibration of harmony and welcome that angels recognize as a reflection of their own love. Gratitude invites angels into the space not merely as distant helpers but as welcomed companions, honored for the wisdom and light they bring.

The intention is now set, a clear and resonant call that reaches outward. With this foundation in place, the ritual becomes an expression of the soul's deepest need, guided by focus and clarity. Each action, whether lighting a candle, saying a prayer, or holding a crystal, is imbued with the energy of the intention, making the ritual a living conversation with the angels. As the practitioner moves through the ritual, they hold this intention in their heart, allowing it to be a constant presence, a soft pulse that guides each word, each gesture, each breath.

As the ritual concludes, the practitioner releases their intention into the universe, trusting that it has reached its destination. This release is as crucial as the setting, for it signals faith and openness, a willingness to allow angels to respond in the way that best serves. Releasing the intention is not an act of letting go but of expanding trust, knowing that the request has been heard and that guidance will come. In this final act, the practitioner steps back, honoring the power of their own intention and the wisdom of the angels, allowing the energy of the ritual to flow freely.

Through the purity of intention, the ritual becomes a bridge between the earthly and divine. It is in this quiet, focused moment that angels draw close, listening and responding, their presence felt as warmth, as light, or as a gentle whisper in the heart. In setting intention, the practitioner has opened a door, an invitation that angels recognize and accept, knowing that they are welcomed and honored in the spirit of true connection.

As intention takes root within the ritual, it transforms from a simple wish into a focused, living force. To strengthen this intention is to refine the energy, allowing it to resonate at a frequency that is both clear and powerful, aligning seamlessly with the angelic realm. The deepening of intention is an art, a practice that draws upon the mind, heart, and spirit in unity. Through techniques such as visualization, affirmation, and emotional attunement, the practitioner builds a bridge between worlds, inviting angels to cross over and make their presence known.

One of the most effective ways to amplify intention is through visualization. This practice, guided by imagination and inner focus, creates a symbolic landscape that the practitioner and angels can share. To begin, one might close the eyes and picture the desire or request as a sphere of radiant light, gently expanding and brightening with each breath. This light, soft and warm, represents the essence of the intention—whether it is a call for guidance, protection, or healing. By visualizing this sphere of light ascending into the spiritual realm, the practitioner sends a clear, vivid message. In this way, visualization is not simply daydreaming; it is a language spoken through images, a language that angels understand and respond to.

Repeating affirmations is another profound method to strengthen intention. Unlike simple statements, these affirmations are infused with the practitioner's faith and focus, transforming words into resonant energies. Phrases such as *"I am open to divine guidance,"* or *"My heart is aligned with angelic wisdom,"* when repeated with sincerity, act as a steady rhythm, harmonizing with the energies the practitioner seeks to connect with. Each repetition engrains the intention deeper within the soul, making it an inseparable part of the practitioner's energetic field. Spoken aloud or within the quiet of the mind, these affirmations shift the practitioner's vibration, aligning it closely with the angelic realm, drawing angels nearer with each word.

For those desiring a more immersive connection, incorporating physical gestures or postures can further enhance intention. Holding the hands over the heart, palms open to the sky, or gently placing a hand on the forehead can ground the intention within the body, symbolizing openness and receptivity. Each gesture serves as a physical manifestation of the inner focus, aligning body and spirit as one. Through these small yet powerful movements, the practitioner reinforces the intention, not only within the mind but within the physical self, becoming an embodiment of the energy they wish to send forth.

Emotion, too, is a vital force that breathes life into intention. The purity and strength of an intention are amplified by the emotions that accompany it. For instance, a request for protection carries a different energy when approached with calm assurance rather than fear. To attune emotions with intention, the practitioner may begin by cultivating a state of gratitude, peace, or love—emotions that resonate at the frequency of angels. By holding this feeling, the practitioner elevates the intention, creating an energetic current that moves swiftly and fluidly toward the realm of angels. When intention and emotion are in harmony, the message sent is unmistakably clear, a vibration angels readily perceive and respond to.

To maintain focus throughout the ritual, a technique known as the "circle of breath" is particularly effective. This practice, involving deep, rhythmic breathing, centers the mind and anchors the intention within each inhalation and exhalation. With each breath drawn in, the practitioner visualizes the intention gathering strength, like a fire kindling, and with each exhale, they release the intention outward, sending it forth into the ether. This circular flow of breath deepens concentration, grounding the practitioner in the present moment while allowing the intention to take on a life of its own, carried by breath into the spiritual realm.

Symbols and images, sacred to the practitioner, can serve as visual anchors for the intention, enhancing focus and clarity. An angelic symbol, a feather, or an image of light can be placed before the practitioner as a reminder of the intention's purpose and power. Gazing upon this symbol throughout the ritual creates a point of connection, a visible reminder that strengthens concentration. This visual focus not only keeps the intention alive but allows it to radiate outward, like ripples in a pond, attracting angelic energies to respond.

Some practitioners may find that writing their intention deepens their focus even further. Taking a moment to write down the desire or request, as if sealing it with the energy of their own hand, holds the intention in the tangible world. This written intention, placed upon an altar, under a crystal, or near a candle, becomes a physical testament to the practitioner's purpose. In this act of writing, the words themselves resonate, the ink becoming a medium through which the intention travels. By placing this written intention in a sacred space, the practitioner reinforces its energy, allowing it to echo into the angelic realm.

Maintaining the strength of intention throughout the ritual involves returning to the original purpose again and again. When the mind begins to drift, a simple touch of the hand to the heart or a soft, quiet whisper of the intention brings the focus back, reconnecting the practitioner to their purpose. These reminders, small and gentle, guide the ritual with a steady rhythm, allowing the intention to remain clear and unbroken. Through this consistency, the practitioner's energy becomes a constant light, a beacon that angels recognize, illuminating the path between worlds.

As the ritual draws to a close, the practitioner gently releases the intention, letting it ascend like a whisper on the wind. This act of release is not an abandonment of the desire but a surrender to the wisdom and timing of the angels. In this letting go, the practitioner signals trust, an openness to receive whatever response the angels may bring. This final act of release holds profound power, as it allows the intention to rise freely, unburdened, flowing into the spiritual realm without resistance.

The ritual completed, the practitioner sits in stillness, embracing a sense of peace and fulfillment. Though the intention is released, its energy remains, woven subtly within the practitioner's own field, a quiet assurance that guidance will come. This quietude, this openness, creates a receptive space within the heart, where the answer may arrive as a feeling, a thought, or even a sign in the days to come.

Thus, the intention set and strengthened becomes more than a request; it is a bridge, a thread of light reaching from earth to the heavens. In this luminous pathway, angels find a welcome, their presence drawn close by the purity and clarity of the intention. And as the practitioner releases the final whisper of the intention into the air, they know they have been heard, surrounded by the quiet assurance that angels have drawn near, ready to respond in their own time and way.

Chapter 6
Meditation for Angelic Connection

Meditation creates a sacred stillness within, a quiet space where the spirit can listen, undistracted, to the whispers of angels. This practice, ancient and timeless, serves as a bridge between realms, calming the mind and opening the heart. By cultivating a state of inner peace and heightened awareness, the practitioner allows angelic energies to flow gently into their life. This meditative approach, when prepared with sincerity and devotion, becomes a welcoming threshold where the voice of the divine may be heard.

To begin, the practitioner finds a place of comfort, a space free from distractions where they can sit or lie in stillness. The surroundings should be calm and clear, perhaps enhanced by soft candlelight or the faint aroma of incense to signal the transition from ordinary time to sacred time. Sitting with a relaxed but upright posture, the practitioner closes their eyes, settling into the quiet. The breath becomes the first focus—a steady, rhythmic anchor that guides the mind away from outer concerns. Inhaling deeply, the practitioner fills the lungs, feeling the expansion, then gently exhales, letting go of any lingering thoughts or emotions. This focus on breath gradually soothes the mind, drawing attention inward.

With each inhalation, the practitioner invites a sense of calm and with each exhalation, they release tension and distraction. This rhythm, simple yet profound, brings the practitioner into a state of centeredness. As the breath deepens, the world outside fades, and the practitioner finds themselves in a space of soft tranquility, where the edges of thought begin to blur and fall away. In this silence, the mind becomes a still lake, undisturbed and reflective, able to receive angelic impressions with clarity.

Once the mind has quieted, the practitioner moves deeper by visualizing a gentle light—a soft, radiant glow—above them. This light, warm and inviting, symbolizes the angelic presence they seek. The light grows brighter, descending slowly until it envelops the practitioner like a cloak, a gentle warmth that surrounds and protects. With each breath, the practitioner visualizes this light permeating their body, filling every cell with peace and purity. This light is not merely imagined; it is felt, a presence that brings comfort and calm. In this sacred light, the practitioner senses that they are not alone but accompanied by angels whose love and protection are as tangible as the breath.

As the light deepens, the practitioner may sense subtle shifts—perhaps a feeling of warmth around the shoulders, a soft tingling on the skin, or a sudden peace that seems to settle within the heart. These sensations, though delicate, are signs of angelic presence, felt rather than seen, experienced as a gentle affirmation that the angels are near. These moments, fleeting yet profound, are not to be forced but allowed, as the practitioner remains in calm observance, trusting that what arises is exactly as it should be. It is in this receptivity, this openness, that angelic messages can flow, reaching the heart directly.

To maintain this connection, the practitioner may use a silent mantra, a word or phrase that resonates with their purpose. Words like *"peace," "light,"* or *"guidance"* can be silently repeated, each repetition deepening the connection. This mantra, simple and unadorned, acts as a steady rhythm that holds the focus, grounding the mind in the present moment. As the practitioner repeats the mantra, it merges with the breath, creating a soft, continuous flow of energy that harmonizes with the angelic realm. The mantra becomes a thread woven into the stillness, gently calling the angels closer, inviting their presence to deepen.

In this quiet state, the practitioner listens—not with the ears, but with the heart. Angelic communication often comes not in words but as a sense, a subtle impression that emerges like a ripple across the still waters of the mind. A feeling of encouragement, a surge of calm, or an intuitive knowing may arise, subtle but unmistakable. These impressions are the language of angels, felt within as a soft illumination, a clarity that carries its own quiet wisdom. The practitioner learns to trust these moments, allowing them to unfold without analysis or doubt. They are received as gifts, precious glimpses into the angelic presence that now gently surrounds.

As the meditation continues, the practitioner remains open, simply allowing the presence of angels to fill the space. There is no urgency, no expectation, only the peaceful awareness of a connection formed in silence. In this sacred stillness, the practitioner may sense the angels as a gentle weight, a subtle warmth, or a deep calm that radiates through the heart. In these moments, time fades, and the practitioner experiences a sense of timelessness, a glimpse into a world that exists beyond the boundaries of thought.

As the meditation draws to a natural close, the practitioner takes a moment to express gratitude, a silent thanks for the angelic presence felt, however fleeting or subtle. Gratitude seals the meditation, creating a gentle resonance that lingers even as the practitioner returns to the world. This gratitude need not be elaborate; it is simply a moment of acknowledgment, a quiet honoring of the angels who have drawn near. In expressing this thanks, the practitioner affirms the bond, knowing that the connection remains even as they return to their day.

The practitioner grounds themselves, bringing awareness back to the body, feeling the connection with the earth beneath them. A few deep breaths reconnect them with the present, and a gentle movement of fingers or toes reminds them of their physical space. Slowly, they open their eyes, carrying with them the calm and presence that the meditation has bestowed. Though the meditation is complete, its essence remains—a soft glow, a subtle strength that lingers, a reminder of the angels whose presence is constant, ready to be felt whenever the heart grows still.

Through this practice, meditation becomes more than a quieting of the mind; it becomes a doorway into communion, a space where the veil thins and the angels draw close. The practitioner, now attuned, carries the resonance of this connection throughout their day, an inner peace, a quiet confidence that the guidance and protection of angels are as close as breath. In this state of calm awareness, the angels remain, ever-present, their whispers heard in the silence that meditation creates, a gentle assurance that they are near, watching, guiding, and holding the soul in light.

For those seeking a deeper connection with angels, meditation expands beyond simplicity, embracing more refined techniques that invite precision and clarity in communion. These advanced practices guide the practitioner further into realms of light, where angelic energies resonate freely. Here, the soul finds itself attuned to an even finer sensitivity, capable of perceiving the quiet movements of angelic presence with an intensity and grace that feels nearly tangible. This journey into profound connection allows the practitioner not only to sense but to experience the presence of angels with a heightened awareness, drawing their guidance ever closer.

To initiate this deeper meditation, the practitioner may begin with a gentle breathing exercise, not just to relax but to elevate the vibrational state. Breathing in through the nose and exhaling softly through the mouth, each breath is visualized as a flow of light entering and exiting the body. The practitioner imagines this light expanding, filling not just the lungs but the entire chest, radiating outward until it forms a cocoon of luminous energy. This cocoon acts as a protective sphere, a sacred space within which only pure angelic energies may enter. The practitioner now sits fully enveloped, safeguarded, and ready to step deeper into the realm of angels.

A guided visualization, one designed to refine attunement, begins with the practitioner imagining a pathway that ascends gently into a landscape of light. This landscape might take the form of a serene, open field bathed in golden rays, or a mountaintop where the air feels pure and vast. With each imagined step, the practitioner feels lighter, as though releasing the weight of earthly concerns, leaving behind any barriers between the self and the angelic presence they seek. As they reach the peak of this inner journey, the practitioner visualizes themselves standing in a radiant, ethereal light, a place where they are at once grounded yet lifted beyond the ordinary.

At this point, the practitioner engages in a specific visualization exercise: the creation of a "meeting place" for angels. This space, envisioned within the mind's eye, serves as a focal point, a sacred ground within the meditation where angels are invited to gather. The practitioner might imagine a glowing circle, lined with light or symbols, where they sit at the center. This circle, drawn mentally with careful intent, becomes a symbolic boundary, a sanctuary that welcomes angels to approach closely, surrounding the practitioner in warmth and protection. Within this space, the atmosphere feels almost alive, tingling with the anticipation of divine presence.

Once the space is established, the practitioner shifts their focus to the heart, the center of emotional resonance and spiritual perception. With each breath, the practitioner imagines a light pulsing from the heart, extending outward in waves, reaching beyond the circle and into the angelic realm. This heart-centered focus is the language angels recognize most clearly, a vibration that speaks directly to their essence. As the practitioner feels this light expand, they may invite a specific angel, perhaps a guardian or a familiar presence, to draw near. This invitation is gentle and unforced, a quiet request held within the heart, opening the door without expectation but with trust.

As the practitioner deepens their state, subtle sensations may begin to arise. A soft warmth across the shoulders, a gentle tingling on the hands, or a light pressure near the forehead may indicate the presence of an angel. These sensations, delicate and almost dreamlike, are the soul's way of perceiving angelic energy, a recognition that cannot be seen but is felt deeply within. Rather than analyzing these impressions, the practitioner allows them to flow, observing and embracing them as signs of connection, knowing that angels communicate through subtlety, a language of sensation and emotion.

Guided meditation and angelic imagery further enhance this connection. The practitioner might envision an angelic figure approaching, surrounded by a shimmering aura, extending a hand or offering a symbol. Whether imagined or felt, these images are profound expressions of communication, carrying meaning that transcends words. The practitioner observes these details, noting colors, gestures, or symbols, all of which carry a message. A feather, a chalice, or even a simple touch on the hand may hold symbolic meaning, insights conveyed in forms the heart intuitively understands. Here, the practitioner finds themselves in a silent dialogue, where images and sensations communicate the angels' wisdom, each one a gentle revelation.

To further align with this presence, sound is a powerful tool. Softly humming a single tone, such as *"ah"* or *"ohm,"* the practitioner resonates with the angelic vibration, merging their voice with the silent frequencies around them. This sound, allowed to flow naturally, holds no form but pure intention, filling the meditative space with a frequency that attracts and anchors angelic energy. Singing bowls, chimes, or even the sound of nature can also amplify this attunement, each vibration clearing and expanding the space, lifting the meditation to new heights of receptivity.

In moments of stillness, the practitioner listens, not expecting words but feeling an inner knowing arise, a clarity that feels both familiar and expansive. Angelic insights often appear as a quiet conviction, a feeling that something is understood deeply without explanation. The practitioner may receive a sense of direction or a peaceful assurance, answers that flow not in sentences but in impressions, each one leaving an imprint upon the heart. In this silence, the practitioner becomes a vessel, holding each message with reverence, knowing that angelic wisdom speaks softly yet profoundly.

As the meditation nears completion, the practitioner gently withdraws their focus from the angelic meeting space, bringing awareness back to the breath and body. In gratitude, they offer a silent thanks, acknowledging the presence and guidance received, however subtle or profound. This gratitude is an essential closing gesture, an honoring of the angels' nearness, a recognition that their presence is not bound by time or place. By offering this thanks, the practitioner seals the meditation, holding the connection close within the heart.

Grounding becomes the final step, a gentle return to the present. The practitioner might visualize roots extending from their feet into the earth, anchoring their energy firmly in the physical world, even as the angelic resonance remains softly within them. Each breath reconnects them, the sense of lightness balanced by the solidity of the earth. When ready, the practitioner opens their eyes, feeling both uplifted and calm, carrying with them a subtle glow, a peace that lingers as a reminder of the communion shared.

Through this deepened meditation, the practitioner finds that angels are not distant but ever near, drawn close through the gentle art of presence and intention. These practices are not mere techniques but gateways, a series of soft openings that allow the divine to touch the human heart. Each meditation becomes a journey, an invitation to step beyond the seen and enter a realm where angels dwell, their presence like a quiet song, a warm light that fills the soul and offers guidance, peace, and love. In this meditative space, the practitioner discovers a truth whispered by angels—a reminder that the divine is always near, a breath away, forever waiting in the stillness for the soul to call.

Chapter 7
Visualization and Tuning

In the quiet depths of visualization, the practitioner finds a pathway into alignment with the angelic realm, a bridge formed not of words but of images, light, and intent. Visualization becomes a powerful tool, enabling the mind to transcend the physical, allowing the heart to reach out across unseen distances to connect with angelic presence. Through this practice, the practitioner shapes mental images, each one a sacred invitation, drawing angels near and amplifying the resonance between human and divine.

As the practitioner begins, they settle into stillness, allowing the mind to quiet and drift toward a space where imagination and spirit meet. Here, the practitioner envisions a place of profound beauty and peace, a sacred landscape crafted from light and intention. This space might appear as a meadow bathed in morning sunlight, a calm ocean under a starlit sky, or a temple glowing softly in the twilight. The chosen setting reflects the practitioner's inner self, a sanctuary where angelic connection feels natural and serene. With each breath, the image grows clearer, more detailed, until it feels alive, a true place of refuge and openness.

In this visualized sanctuary, the practitioner creates a focal point, a center where the angelic presence is welcomed. This might take the form of a glowing altar, a circle of light, or an archway, each symbolizing an opening through which angels may step. Within this space, the practitioner holds their intention—their purpose for the connection. Whether it is to seek guidance, feel protected, or simply to commune in silence, this intention fills the air, resonating softly throughout the visualization.

As the image stabilizes, the practitioner turns their focus to summoning light, the universal language of the angelic realm. This light, imagined as radiant and warm, begins to flow down from above, illuminating the sanctuary and filling it with a gentle glow. The practitioner visualizes this light as it expands, growing brighter, embracing every part of the scene, inviting the angels to approach. This light becomes a bridge, a radiant stream that angels may follow, drawn by its purity and by the practitioner's heartfelt invitation. In this glow, a feeling of peace and warmth emerges, and the sense of angelic presence begins to awaken within the space.

The practitioner now visualizes specific symbols associated with angels, each one a key that opens the doorway further. These symbols may be as simple as feathers drifting softly through the air, or as intricate as angelic sigils, crosses, or rays of light extending in gentle arcs. Each symbol, held with reverence, carries a meaning and energy that aligns with the practitioner's purpose. For example, a feather represents grace and protection, while a beam of light embodies divine wisdom. As each symbol takes shape within the mind, the space becomes alive with a language beyond words—a language of images that angels understand instinctively.

With each symbol, the practitioner's awareness deepens, allowing them to feel the texture of angelic energy—soft yet powerful, gentle yet infinitely vast. The visualization process is now like a silent dialogue, where each symbol and image acts as a gesture of openness, an invitation to connect. In this dialogue, angels respond not with words but with sensations—a feeling of warmth, a deep calm, or an overwhelming sense of lightness. These sensations affirm their presence, a reassurance that they have crossed the bridge, that they are near, watching and listening.

The practitioner may now choose to visualize themselves standing before an angelic figure, a being of pure light who extends warmth and guidance. This angel appears as a luminous presence, with features gently defined by the glow surrounding them, embodying an energy that feels familiar and comforting. This visualization allows the practitioner to feel the closeness of angelic presence, as though they were standing side by side with a being who understands and cares deeply. In this moment, the practitioner can silently share thoughts or questions, sending them out into the light, knowing that this angelic figure hears and understands.

To deepen the connection further, the practitioner might engage in a practice called "tuning"—the act of harmonizing one's own energy with the angelic frequency. Tuning involves visualizing the self as a clear vessel, filled only with light and openness. By breathing deeply, the practitioner attunes their energy field to the frequency of love, peace, and clarity, matching the vibrations of the angelic realm. Each breath is imagined as a wave, clearing away all distractions, allowing only the most elevated energy to remain. As the practitioner reaches this state of tuning, they feel a profound resonance, as though they and the angelic beings are vibrating at the same frequency, united in purpose and presence.

As the meditation draws to a close, the practitioner gently releases the visualization, watching as the sacred symbols, the sanctuary, and the angelic figure fade into soft light. This release is intentional, a respectful conclusion that acknowledges the connection while allowing it to dissolve naturally. Before returning fully to the present, the practitioner takes a moment of gratitude, sending silent thanks to the angels for their presence. This gratitude is a powerful grounding force, a recognition of the sacred exchange that has taken place.

Opening the eyes, the practitioner finds that the experience lingers—a subtle glow, a gentle feeling of peace that remains as a reminder of the connection. Though the visualization has ended, the presence of the angels endures, a quiet assurance that they remain close, their guidance only a thought away. This practice, repeated and refined, becomes a bridge that grows stronger with each use, a familiar path that the heart knows, where angels wait, ready to offer their light. Through visualization and tuning, the practitioner has not only connected but has become a part of the angelic presence, carrying its resonance into the rhythms of everyday life, a silent, unbreakable bond between realms.

As the practitioner becomes more comfortable with visualization, the practice deepens, evolving into a refined art that amplifies their bond with angels. This enhanced tuning goes beyond the initial steps, delving into advanced visualization techniques that create a sacred, shared meeting space where angels are invited to draw close. Each image, each detail of this spiritual landscape, is imbued with intention, forming a magnetic energy that resonates within the angelic realm.

To begin, the practitioner settles into stillness, breathing deeply, and allowing the mind to quiet. They then envision themselves within a vast, luminous sanctuary—an ethereal realm where time fades, and only the pure presence of light remains. This sacred space might take many forms: a celestial garden, a shimmering temple, or an infinite field of starlight. The practitioner envisions each detail with clarity and reverence, forming a mental image that feels alive, as though stepping into a realm beyond the ordinary. This image is not static; it breathes with light, creating a foundation where angels feel welcome.

The next step involves constructing a focal point within this sacred space—a radiant circle or an altar of light where the practitioner may sit or stand. This focal point is an intentional space of invitation, a gateway through which angels may pass. Visualizing this circle as glowing and soft, the practitioner fills it with symbols of peace, such as flowers, candles, or crystals, each symbol chosen with care to represent openness and readiness for communion. The practitioner takes a few breaths, centering themselves within this circle, grounding their energy, and focusing on the intention to connect with the angelic realm.

At this stage, the practitioner enhances the visualization by imagining angelic symbols radiating around them. These symbols—feathers, light-filled wings, or radiant orbs—are imagined floating gently in the air, carrying energies of peace, wisdom, and protection. Each symbol is crafted with the practitioner's purpose in mind, aligning with their intention for the meditation. A feather may signify guidance, a light beam may represent healing, and a crystal form may embody clarity. These symbols surround the practitioner, each one vibrating with angelic frequency, amplifying the sacred atmosphere and creating an energetic bridge.

A profound technique that furthers tuning is the visualization of angelic sigils or sacred geometries, drawn with light within the mind's eye. The practitioner may trace an angelic sigil—a symbol uniquely linked to an archangel or a protective spirit—within their sacred space, visualizing it glowing and pulsing gently. As each sigil is visualized, it becomes a direct call, a silent request that angels respond to instinctively. Each line and curve of the symbol carries an energy that aligns with the angelic realm, like a beacon of light guiding the angels to this consecrated space.

The practitioner now moves to harmonize their own energy with this visualization through "light breathing," a practice that unites breath with imagery. As they inhale, they imagine breathing in pure, radiant light from the circle around them, filling their body and aura with this high frequency. On each exhale, they visualize this light expanding, merging with the angelic symbols and filling the sacred space with an even brighter glow. With every breath, the practitioner's energy becomes more synchronized with the angelic vibration, tuning their own aura to resonate in harmony with the presence they wish to connect with.

In this state of attunement, the practitioner may feel subtle shifts—a warmth in the hands, a gentle tingling along the spine, or a feeling of weightlessness that suggests an angelic presence drawing near. These sensations, delicate yet unmistakable, indicate that the boundary between realms is fading, allowing angels to approach. Rather than analyzing these impressions, the practitioner remains in a state of quiet receptivity, allowing the experience to unfold naturally. Each sensation is a sign, a gentle affirmation of the angels' presence within the sacred space.

For those who wish to deepen this tuning even further, visualizing a "meeting place" within the heart becomes a powerful practice. The practitioner envisions a small sanctuary within the heart—a chamber filled with golden light, calm and pure, where angels may enter to commune more intimately. This space within the heart is imagined as a quiet, boundless room, filled with warmth, where the practitioner and angels may share a moment of deep connection. Visualizing this space with detail and clarity, the practitioner silently invites the angels to step within, feeling a gentle expansion in the chest as this inner door opens.

To solidify this connection, the practitioner can visualize themselves and the angels exchanging symbols of light—a gesture of trust and unity. The practitioner imagines offering a small token, perhaps a crystal or a candle of light, to the angels, who in return extend a symbol back. This exchange is subtle but profound, a shared gesture that signifies mutual respect and recognition. As the practitioner receives the angelic symbol, they feel its energy merging with their own, enhancing their sense of peace, love, or clarity.

As the visualization begins to draw to a close, the practitioner gently allows the symbols and images to dissolve, returning their focus to the breath. They watch as the sacred space fades softly, leaving only the sense of angelic presence lingering within. This process of release is intentional and respectful, an acknowledgment that the connection remains even as the imagery fades. Before concluding, the practitioner offers a quiet moment of gratitude, sending thanks to the angels for their presence, their guidance, and the light they have shared. This gratitude seals the visualization, grounding the experience within the heart.

Returning to the present, the practitioner opens their eyes, carrying the calm and resonance of the experience into their day. Though the sacred space was created in the mind, its effects are felt deeply, a reminder that the angels are close, accessible through a quiet moment of focus and visualization. This practice, repeated and refined, becomes a doorway that the heart instinctively knows, a path where angels wait, ready to respond to the call of light.

Through advanced visualization and tuning, the practitioner learns to weave a sanctuary within, where angels are welcomed not as distant beings but as trusted companions. The sacred space remains, a hidden refuge where divine connection is both real and profound. Each session strengthens this bridge, enabling the practitioner to carry the resonance of angelic presence as a quiet light within, a silent assurance that guidance and protection are always near, ready to answer whenever the soul reaches out.

Chapter 8
Basic Invocation

In the act of invocation, the practitioner speaks across the boundary between worlds, opening a channel for angelic energies to flow into their life. A basic invocation, when performed with sincerity and clarity, acts as a beacon, guiding angels to the one who calls with a sense of purpose and reverence..

To begin, the practitioner sets a calm atmosphere, grounding themselves in a quiet space where distractions fall away. The act of invoking angels is both simple and profound, requiring no elaborate language but only a heart-centered focus and a genuine desire to connect. As they settle into a calm state, the practitioner may place a hand over the heart, feeling each beat as a reminder of the purity and truth behind the call. This touch grounds the practitioner, aligning their intentions with the realm they wish to reach, creating a point of stillness and sincerity from which the invocation can rise.

The words chosen for invocation need not be complex. In fact, the most effective invocations are often the simplest, speaking directly from the heart to the angels with honesty and humility. A basic invocation might be as simple as: *"Angels of light, I call upon you. I ask for your presence, your guidance, and your protection."* This straightforward request opens the way, inviting angelic presence without adornment, creating an energetic space where angels may enter freely. With each word, the practitioner releases intention, transforming it into a thread of light that angels perceive and follow.

Tone and rhythm are essential, as the voice itself carries energy that resonates beyond spoken words. Speaking slowly, with clear articulation, allows the intention to move gently, almost as if each word itself is a prayer. The practitioner's voice becomes a vessel, each sound aligning with the higher frequencies of the angelic realm. To invoke angels is to invite them not only through words but through the quality of voice, a tone that carries respect, clarity, and peace. This rhythm forms a steady flow, like a river drawing light from one realm to the next, creating a sacred bridge.

The practitioner may choose to enhance the invocation by holding a specific gesture, such as open hands or a gentle bow of the head, symbolizing openness and humility. This gesture reflects the inner intention physically, signaling to the angels that the heart is open and ready to receive. Open palms, facing upward, mirror a gesture of acceptance, an invitation for guidance and blessings to descend. In this moment, the body, mind, and voice are unified, each one contributing to the sincerity of the call.

Visualizing a sphere of light surrounding them further strengthens the invocation, as this light serves as both a protective space and a beacon. The practitioner imagines this light gently expanding with each word spoken, creating a sphere that glows brighter and purer as the invocation continues. This light, radiant and warm, is imagined filling the space, creating an environment where angels may enter without obstruction. As this sphere of light surrounds the practitioner, they feel shielded, embraced in a sacred space that allows angelic energies to come close, responding to the call in safety and peace.

As the invocation continues, the practitioner may sense a subtle shift—a feeling of calm, a warmth on the skin, or a deep inner peace that signals the presence of angels. These sensations are not forced but allowed, appearing as gentle confirmations of the connection. With the invocation complete, the practitioner rests in silence, allowing the energy to settle, letting the words and intentions resonate outward. This pause is essential, a quiet moment where the call is released, like a feather drifting gently on the air, carrying the practitioner's intention toward the angelic realm.

If the practitioner feels moved to elaborate, they may offer a brief and specific request, framed with clarity and respect. For example, *"I ask for your guidance in times of doubt,"* or *"I invite your protection in this place of peace."* Such requests remain concise, focusing on a single intention rather than multiple desires. This clarity sharpens the energy of the invocation, allowing it to reach directly to the angels, undiluted by complex wording. Angels respond to sincerity more than detail; thus, each phrase is a heartfelt whisper that rises simply, yet powerfully.

Closing the invocation is as important as beginning it. The practitioner may offer a short phrase of gratitude, such as *"Thank you for your presence and your guidance."* This gratitude acts as a seal, closing the invocation with respect and acknowledging the angels' response, whatever form it may take. By giving thanks, the practitioner solidifies the connection, signaling the completion of the call while trusting that the guidance or protection invited will follow in due time.

The final act of release allows the invocation to rise freely, without attachment or expectation. The practitioner lets go of any specific outcome, trusting that the angels will respond in alignment with what serves the highest good. This release shows faith in the process, an understanding that the call has been heard and will be answered in a way that honors the practitioner's path. With this surrender, the practitioner's role becomes one of openness and readiness to receive, a state that angels recognize and respond to with grace.

In the quiet that follows, the practitioner may feel a sense of calm assurance, a silent confirmation that the connection remains, woven softly into the fabric of their day. The words spoken linger, their resonance a reminder that angels are near, drawn close by the simplicity and purity of a sincere call. This practice of invocation, though basic in structure, holds within it the essence of communion, a gentle opening that allows angels to approach with light, protection, and wisdom.

Through this practice, invocation becomes a doorway that the practitioner may return to, each call creating a thread of light that weaves connection between realms. In each invocation, the bond strengthens, and the practitioner learns to trust that even the simplest words hold the power to summon angels, to welcome them with reverence, and to feel their presence as a quiet, guiding force woven into every moment.

As the practitioner grows familiar with the sacred act of invocation, they may begin to explore more detailed methods that intensify the call, drawing angels closer and enhancing the energy of their presence. This deepening of invocation is a practice of both focus and reverence, where each word, gesture, and intention becomes an offering. Here, the practitioner learns how specific words, tones, and gestures shape the energy of the call, resonating in harmony with the angelic realm.

To prepare, the practitioner sets a quiet space, creating an atmosphere of stillness that is both welcoming and intentional. A candle may be lit to symbolize the purity of the invocation, its flame acting as a beacon that guides angels to the place where they are invited. With the gentle glow illuminating the room, the practitioner centers their thoughts, breathing deeply to settle the mind and heart into a unified focus. The intention here is to invoke angels with clarity and respect, using both voice and energy as instruments of the call.

As they begin, the practitioner may choose a structured invocation, crafted to enhance each word's impact. The language of invocation is simple yet powerful; it is direct but imbued with reverence. For example, the practitioner might say: *"Angels of light, protectors of peace, I humbly invite your presence. Surround me with your guidance and your strength. I call upon you with gratitude and trust."* Each phrase is spoken slowly, with mindful articulation, allowing the energy of each word to rise and resonate. These words, carefully chosen, create a rhythm, like a song sung in honor of the angels, filled with both humility and sincerity.

The practitioner may amplify this call by visualizing angelic symbols or envisioning a specific archangel or guardian in the room. By focusing on a name or symbol that resonates deeply, such as the symbol of a feather or a radiant star, the practitioner sharpens their intent, crafting a distinct invitation that angels can clearly perceive. This visualization, held firmly within the mind, serves as a guidepost, creating a path of light that angels may follow. In this heightened state of awareness, the symbols feel almost tangible, woven into the air, creating a sacred threshold where angels are welcomed.

A gentle but powerful addition to invocation is the use of sacred gestures, such as bringing the hands together in prayer or extending them upward, palms open to receive. Each gesture embodies the openness and readiness to connect, signaling to the angels that the practitioner is fully present and receptive. These gestures, performed with calm intention, ground the invocation within the body, making it a full expression of heart, mind, and spirit. When the hands are opened, the practitioner feels a current of energy flowing through them, a subtle vibration that extends outward, becoming a bridge between the earthly and angelic realms.

For those seeking to raise the energetic frequency of the call, the use of tone and vocal vibration serves as a powerful tool. Certain vocal tones, such as the soft hum of *"Ah"* or the clear sound of *"Ohm,"* resonate with the angelic frequency, creating waves of energy that purify the space. The practitioner may chant softly, allowing the sound to vibrate through the body and into the surrounding space. Each tone carries a purity that aligns with the essence of angels, creating a field of resonance where their presence is naturally drawn. In this chant, the voice becomes an instrument, a vessel of light that angels recognize and respond to instinctively.

To deepen the invocation further, the practitioner may construct a short invocation prayer that raises the tone and vibration to ensure that the call is heard. This prayer, designed with care, brings together all elements of the invocation—voice, gesture, intention, and visualization—into a single expression of connection. For instance: *"Angels of light, guardians of the path, I call upon you with an open heart. Guide me with wisdom, protect me with grace, and surround me with your healing light."* Each line of the prayer flows naturally, spoken in a tone that is both commanding and reverent, echoing with an energy that transcends words.

With the prayer complete, the practitioner then pauses, allowing a moment of stillness where the words can resonate outward. This silence is intentional, a space of openness where the energy of the call is free to rise and reach the angelic realm. In this stillness, the practitioner listens, not expecting a response but allowing for the subtle sensations of angelic presence to be felt. These sensations may come as a warmth around the shoulders, a quiet sense of peace, or a sudden clarity within the mind. Each feeling is a sign, a soft indication that the angels have heard and are near, responding in their own silent, luminous way.

A final element that deepens the invocation is the expression of gratitude, spoken as a concluding gesture that acknowledges the angels' presence and support. The practitioner may say, *"Thank you, angels, for your guidance and light. I trust in your presence and your love."* This gratitude serves as both a closing and a grounding, anchoring the energy of the invocation within the heart. Through this simple act of thanks, the practitioner acknowledges the sacred exchange, affirming that the connection is complete yet ongoing, woven into the fabric of their life.

As the invocation concludes, the practitioner takes a few moments to remain in quiet reflection, feeling the presence of the angels surrounding them. This stillness allows the energy of the invocation to settle, grounding it within both body and spirit. The practitioner then releases the invocation, letting go of any expectations, trusting that the angels will respond in a manner that aligns with divine timing and purpose. In this release, the practitioner demonstrates faith, knowing that the call has been heard and that guidance will come in its own way.

With each repetition of this practice, the bond between the practitioner and the angelic realm grows stronger. The invocation becomes a familiar path, a ritual of light that the practitioner can return to in moments of need, comfort, or gratitude. Over time, the practitioner learns that invocation is more than a call—it is a profound communion, a dance between worlds, where angels draw near not as distant beings but as present guides and protectors.

Through these advanced techniques, the practice of invocation transforms, becoming a channel through which angelic energy flows freely, filling the practitioner's life with clarity, protection, and peace. This connection, nurtured by sincerity and reverence, is a source of inner strength, a reminder that angels are always close, ready to respond, waiting only for the quiet, heartfelt call of the soul.

Chapter 9
Incense and Herbs for Connection

The aroma of incense and the subtle energy of herbs have long been used as sacred tools to elevate the spirit, purify space, and invite divine presence. In angelic rituals, these elements play an essential role, preparing an atmosphere where the veil between realms thins and the presence of angels can be sensed. Each herb, each waft of smoke, resonates at a frequency that aligns with angelic energy, allowing the practitioner to create a space where connection flows naturally.

To begin, the practitioner selects incense or herbs with specific properties that enhance spiritual receptivity. Certain traditional choices, such as frankincense, myrrh, sage, and sandalwood, have been valued across cultures for their ability to elevate the spirit and clear energy. Frankincense, with its warm and resinous scent, has long been associated with purification and the calling of higher energies, creating a sacred atmosphere where angels feel invited. Myrrh, a scent both grounding and mystical, is known for its ability to protect and connect, offering a sense of depth and tranquility. Each fragrance, chosen with intention, becomes a note in a symphony that resonates with the angelic realm.

The ritual begins with the practitioner preparing the space, holding the chosen incense or herbs with reverence, understanding that each one carries its own spirit and energy. Lighting the incense becomes an act of dedication, a gentle gesture that signals the opening of sacred space. As the smoke begins to rise, curling softly and filling the room, it moves as a bridge, a mist that gently dissolves the boundaries between worlds. The practitioner watches this movement, allowing their mind to soften and expand, feeling each breath filled with the purity of the aroma. The smoke, both physical and ethereal, serves as a channel, a means by which angels are drawn near, carried by the invitation embedded within the scent.

Sage, particularly revered for its cleansing properties, is often used at the beginning of the ritual to clear the space of any residual energies. The practitioner may walk slowly through the room, allowing the smoke to reach each corner, visualizing any dense or lingering energies dissolving. This ritual of cleansing opens the room to higher frequencies, leaving it receptive and pure, creating a space that welcomes only light. In this clarity, the energy feels lighter, more spacious, a sanctuary where angels feel comfortable and the practitioner feels a sense of peace.

After cleansing, the practitioner may turn to herbs or incense specifically chosen to attract angelic presence. Sandalwood, known for its grounding yet uplifting qualities, is particularly powerful in aligning the practitioner's energy with higher realms. Its scent brings a sense of inner calm, allowing the practitioner to release stress and focus deeply on their connection with angels. Holding a small dish or stick of sandalwood incense, the practitioner breathes in slowly, visualizing each breath as an opening, an invitation that reaches across dimensions. In this way, the scent becomes more than an aroma; it is a language, a silent call that angels recognize and respond to.

For those wishing to deepen the ritual, combining several herbs creates a blend that harmonizes energies, amplifying the effect. A small bundle or incense blend of frankincense, lavender, and cedar, for example, brings together the qualities of purity, peace, and protection. Frankincense purifies, lavender calms and aligns, and cedar grounds and protects, each element contributing to a balanced environment where the practitioner can feel secure in the connection. As the practitioner lights this blend, the combined smoke rises as a single stream, symbolizing unity, the merging of energies that invite angels with warmth and grace.

Beyond the smoke, dried herbs may also be placed on an altar or within the sacred space as symbols of the invitation. A small bowl of lavender or a single sprig of rosemary acts as a silent call, each plant chosen for its own unique frequency. Lavender, gentle and calming, soothes the mind, creating a peaceful energy that angels naturally resonate with. Rosemary, with its invigorating fragrance, serves as a protector, strengthening the intention of the ritual and ensuring that the space remains sacred and undisturbed. Each herb, though simple, carries within it an ancient wisdom, a natural vibration that aligns with the purity of angelic realms.

The practitioner may deepen their connection by incorporating the act of consecration, blessing the incense or herbs before they are used. Holding the incense in their hands, the practitioner may close their eyes and set a clear intention: *"May this incense purify, uplift, and invite the presence of angels."* This consecration transforms the herb or incense into more than a tool; it becomes an ally, a part of the ritual that holds the practitioner's intention and carries it outward. With each blessing, the practitioner's intention merges with the natural essence of the incense, creating a resonance that angels feel as a genuine invitation.

As the ritual continues, the practitioner allows themselves to become fully immersed in the sensory experience, feeling the aroma flow through the room and into the spirit. Each inhalation brings a sense of calm, each waft of smoke a reminder of the angels' nearness. In this heightened awareness, the practitioner may feel subtle shifts—the air growing lighter, a sensation of warmth, or a quiet peace that seems to envelop the space. These sensations, delicate and reassuring, are signs of angelic presence, felt through the invisible language of scent and energy.

When the ritual concludes, the practitioner offers gratitude for the herbs and incense, acknowledging their role in creating a sacred bridge. Extinguishing the incense is done with respect, allowing the smoke to fade gently, carrying the energy of the ritual upward. This closing act honors the connection that has been made, sealing the ritual in peace. The practitioner then sits for a few quiet moments, breathing in any lingering fragrance, feeling the serenity that remains—a reminder that angels are close, their presence woven subtly into the air.

Through the art of incense and herbs, the practitioner learns that angelic connection is not only about words or prayers but about the quiet partnership with nature's elements. Each fragrance becomes a language, a message of peace that angels recognize and answer, drawn near by the purity of the invitation. This connection, grounded in the simple act of lighting incense, becomes a way to carry the angels' presence into everyday life, a reminder that they are always near, responding to the soft call of scent and spirit.

As the practitioner's understanding of incense and herbs deepens, the use of these elements becomes a refined art, tailored to amplify angelic communication. Beyond single herbs or simple incense, the practitioner learns to create specific blends and employ consecration practices that heighten spiritual receptivity, making each ritual richer and more profound. Through careful selection, blending, and activation, the practitioner aligns their space and energy, drawing angelic presence even closer, with scents and herbs woven thoughtfully to form an intricate language of invitation.

The practice of blending herbs and incense creates a more personalized and potent ritual atmosphere. The practitioner might begin by selecting herbs not only for their known spiritual properties but for the unique ways they blend together. For instance, a mix of frankincense for purification, cedar for grounding, and rose for love forms a harmonious blend that both protects and invites angelic energies associated with comfort and guidance. Each herb chosen contributes its distinct essence, but combined, they create an atmosphere attuned to specific spiritual needs.

To prepare these blends, the practitioner may crush dried herbs gently with a mortar and pestle, focusing on each herb's contribution to the whole. As the herbs are ground, a simple intention is set, such as, "May these herbs unify to create a sanctuary of peace and divine presence." This blending becomes an act of devotion, each motion a reminder of the intention for angelic connection. As the crushed herbs release their fragrance, the practitioner senses the power of the blend strengthening, creating an energetic synergy that angels are drawn to recognize.

With the blend prepared, the practitioner may further elevate its purpose through consecration—imbuing the herbs with the practitioner's specific intention. Consecration transforms the blend from a physical tool to a sacred vessel of energy. To consecrate the incense or herbs, the practitioner holds the blend in both hands, closing their eyes, and visualizes a soft golden light infusing the mix, carrying their prayer and purpose. This light serves as a protective energy, wrapping around each particle, readying it for ritual use. A few words of consecration, such as "By this light, I dedicate these herbs to the purpose of divine communion," finalize the blessing, sealing the energy within the blend.

Once consecrated, the practitioner can choose to burn the herbs as loose incense on charcoal or to create small herbal bundles, each tailored to specific invocations or moments of reflection. When lit, the smoke rises, carrying the consecrated intention with it, lifting the prayer to the angelic realm. As the practitioner watches the smoke rise, they may focus on their specific request or intention, feeling the blend acting as a messenger, reaching out across the unseen to the angels with clarity and purpose.

Methods to activate and intensify the intention within the herbs through affirmations and visualization can be applied as the incense or herbal blend burns. The practitioner might quietly repeat affirmations such as, "This space is now blessed and open to divine connection," or "Angelic light surrounds and protects." Each repetition strengthens the energetic effect, merging sound with scent, creating a powerful resonance that angels feel as an open call. The practitioner may visualize the smoke swirling gently, forming a luminous thread connecting the earthly space with the higher realm, a pathway on which angels travel to respond to the call.

Herbal blends also lend themselves to the creation of sacred sachets or amulets, which can act as ongoing sources of connection. A small pouch filled with a specific combination of herbs, crystals, and perhaps a written invocation may be placed on an altar, worn, or carried. These sachets act as portable sanctuaries, holding the energy of connection wherever the practitioner goes. For example, a sachet containing lavender, rose petals, and angelica root may be created as a token of angelic protection, a small but powerful reminder of the presence and comfort that angels bring.

In addition to blends and sachets, the practitioner may create herbal-infused oils or water for use in anointing spaces, objects, or even themselves. Anointing with these infused oils brings the angelic connection directly to the practitioner's aura, allowing them to carry the energy with them throughout the day. To create an anointing oil, the practitioner might place dried herbs—such as rosemary for clarity and myrrh for grounding—into a base oil, setting it aside in a warm place for several days. This process, done with focused intention, infuses the oil with the spiritual qualities of the herbs, creating a potent tool that brings angelic connection close. When applied with reverence, the oil serves as both protection and invitation, signaling to angels that they are welcome to draw near.

As the practitioner explores these advanced techniques, they may wish to enhance their awareness of the subtle energies that herbs and incense evoke. During the ritual, the practitioner sits quietly, becoming attuned to the subtle shifts within the space, observing changes in temperature, lightness, or peace. These are the echoes of angelic presence, felt through the sensory language that herbs and incense make possible. Through this heightened awareness, the practitioner senses that the angels have responded, subtly altering the room's atmosphere, creating a sanctuary where they may linger in silence and grace.

To complete and close the session, a grounding ritual is practiced. As the incense or herbs burn low, the practitioner takes a moment to express gratitude to the angels, the herbs, and the spirit of connection created. This gratitude grounds the experience, allowing the energy to settle and integrate. Extinguishing the herbs or incense with respect, the practitioner sits in reflection, feeling the lingering effects of the ritual, aware that the energy of connection remains woven into their space and spirit.

Through the art of blending, consecrating, and activating herbs and incense, the practitioner learns that angelic communication is multi-layered, a communion that engages all senses and heightens awareness. These elements, simple yet profound, become allies in the journey of divine connection, each ritual building upon the last, each blend an invitation for angels to step closer. In this practice, the practitioner discovers that angels are near, listening and watching, drawn by the gentle call of scent and smoke, their presence a steady and enduring light that remains.

Chapter 10
Crystals for Angelic Communication

Crystals, revered across traditions for their grounding and transformative qualities, serve as powerful conduits for angelic energy, amplifying the practitioner's connection to the spiritual realm. Each crystal holds unique properties, resonating at frequencies that invite different aspects of angelic presence, from protection to healing and guidance. When incorporated into angelic rituals, these natural allies become energetic bridges, creating a heightened environment where communication with angels can flourish.

The practitioner begins by selecting crystals that align with their intention. Certain stones are traditionally recognized for their effectiveness in angelic connection, each resonating with specific energies that facilitate spiritual receptivity. Clear quartz, known as the "Master Healer," amplifies energy and purifies the space, making it ideal for any angelic communication. Its clarity sharpens intention, allowing messages to flow freely. Celestite, with its soft blue glow, is often called the "Stone of Heaven." Its energy is gentle yet potent, enhancing peace and opening channels to higher realms, making it particularly suited for those seeking guidance from guardian angels. Rose quartz, symbolizing unconditional love, creates an aura of warmth and compassion, allowing the practitioner to feel enveloped in the embrace of angelic presence.

Once the crystals are chosen, the practitioner prepares them by cleansing and dedicating them specifically for angelic connection. This cleansing may be done with smoke, sunlight, or by placing the crystals under moonlight to absorb and radiate pure energy. As the practitioner gently waves incense smoke over the crystals or places them in sunlight, they set a clear intention: *"May these crystals hold only energies of love, light, and connection with the angelic realm."* This dedication ensures that the crystals are ready to amplify only positive and harmonious vibrations, preparing them to act as focused conduits of divine energy.

With cleansed and dedicated crystals, the practitioner arranges them within the sacred space or holds them directly during the ritual. For enhanced connection, crystals can be placed around the practitioner in a gentle circle, symbolizing a protected sphere of light. This placement creates a secure boundary where angelic presence feels welcomed, providing a sanctuary that aligns both the energy of the crystals and the practitioner's intentions. The stones become silent sentinels, anchoring the space with steady energy that allows the practitioner to feel grounded, calm, and receptive to angelic messages.

To amplify the energetic resonance of the crystals, the practitioner may program each one with a specific purpose. By holding the crystal close to the heart, they focus on their intention, such as *"I program this quartz to guide me to clarity in my connection with angels,"* or *"I dedicate this celestite to open my spirit to receive messages of peace."* This intentional programming fine-tunes the crystal's frequency, aligning it directly with the practitioner's purpose. In essence, each crystal becomes a specialized tool, amplifying the energy required for the unique needs of the ritual, whether that is guidance, protection, or healing.

During the ritual, the practitioner might hold a crystal in each hand, or place one over the heart or third-eye chakra, to enhance receptivity. The weight of the stones serves as a grounding force, drawing the practitioner's awareness inward, while their subtle vibrations elevate the mind and heart. As the practitioner sits in stillness, feeling the gentle warmth of the crystal's energy, they may sense a softening in the boundaries of consciousness, an openness that allows angelic energies to draw closer. Crystals like amethyst, with its deep purple hue and calming properties, are especially powerful when placed over the third eye, encouraging inner vision and helping to perceive angelic messages as clear, intuitive insights.

Visualization complements the work with crystals, strengthening the connection further. The practitioner imagines the chosen crystal glowing with a radiant light, its energy expanding to fill the room, creating a luminous sphere that welcomes angelic presence. This light, steady and pure, forms a bridge, a beacon that reaches beyond the physical realm. With each breath, the practitioner envisions the light growing stronger, until it is a soft, shimmering field that invites angels to approach. This visualization enhances the crystal's natural properties, creating a magnetic field that resonates at the frequency of angelic realms.

In the heightened atmosphere created by crystals, the practitioner may begin to sense subtle shifts—an increase in warmth, a tingling sensation, or a feeling of tranquility that envelops the space. These sensations serve as gentle affirmations of angelic presence, a response to the call amplified by the crystals. The practitioner remains open, observing these subtle signs as messages, feeling that the angels are near, their energy seamlessly blending with the crystal's vibration to create a field of unity.

Once the ritual is complete, the practitioner offers a moment of gratitude, honoring both the angelic presence and the crystals as sacred tools in the connection. Each crystal is carefully placed back onto the altar or in a safe space, acknowledging the energy it has shared. As a closing gesture, the practitioner may say, *"Thank you for your light, your guidance, and your presence. I release you with gratitude and peace."* This act of release respects the energy shared, allowing the angelic and earthly energies to return gently to their natural states.

Through this practice, the use of crystals becomes more than a simple ritual element; it becomes a trusted method for establishing consistent and deepening connection with angels. Each crystal holds within it the memory of intention, the imprint of purpose, creating a cumulative effect that strengthens with every ritual. Over time, the practitioner learns that the crystals are not just tools, but allies, quiet and powerful, reflecting the stability and purity of the angelic presence they seek to invoke.

In each ritual, the crystal's energy and the practitioner's intention weave together, forming a harmonious field where angelic connection thrives, and where messages of light, love, and peace can be received as naturally as a heartbeat. This practice reminds the practitioner that just as crystals carry energy from the earth, angels carry energy from the divine, and within this union lies a pathway to enduring guidance and grace.

As the practitioner's connection with crystals deepens, their understanding of these tools evolves, uncovering advanced techniques that amplify the interaction between crystal energy and angelic realms. This progression introduces practices of crystal positioning, programming, and harmonizing, each of which elevates the vibration of the ritual space and intensifies the angelic bond. Through intentional placement and tuning, crystals become vessels that not only attract angelic energies but also sustain the connection, creating an environment where divine messages are clearer and more immediate.

To begin, the practitioner arranges crystals with deliberate focus, positioning them in specific patterns known for their ability to magnify spiritual energies. Crystals placed in a circular formation, for example, create a sanctuary of balanced energy, symbolizing protection and unity. In this circle, a larger stone—such as clear quartz—might be positioned at the center as an amplifier, with smaller stones, like celestite, amethyst, or rose quartz, radiating outward. Each crystal within this arrangement contributes to a unified field that amplifies the presence of angels, creating a subtle yet powerful current where divine energies flow naturally toward the center, enveloping the practitioner.

Another positioning technique includes using a triangle formation with points representing specific aspects of connection.

For instance, placing three crystals—one for protection, one for clarity, and one for guidance—at each point of a triangle directs and refines the energy within. This layout allows the practitioner to focus on distinct qualities while simultaneously invoking a harmonious angelic presence. Positioned within this formation, the practitioner sits at the heart of a vibrational matrix that elevates and aligns their energy with that of the angelic realm, allowing for an immersive experience where angelic communication is felt as a living presence.

With the crystals set, the practitioner moves to the practice of advanced programming, tuning each crystal to specific angelic frequencies. This process involves quieting the mind and focusing on the unique purpose each crystal will serve in the ritual. Holding a crystal, such as amethyst, the practitioner visualizes it glowing with a color or symbol that embodies its role, saying, *"I program this crystal to bring clarity and enhance my vision of angelic guidance."* By doing this, the crystal's natural properties are aligned with the practitioner's intention, sharpening its effectiveness as a channel for receiving messages. Each crystal, programmed with intent, becomes a finely tuned instrument, working harmoniously to support the specific focus of the ritual.

The practitioner may take this practice further by dedicating specific crystals to particular angels, creating a personal connection with these divine beings. This dedication might involve calling upon Archangel Michael, known for his protective qualities, while holding a grounding stone like black tourmaline or smoky quartz. The practitioner might say, *"Archangel Michael, I dedicate this crystal to serve as a beacon of your protection and strength."* This dedication imbues the crystal with the energy of the archangel, creating a bridge between the practitioner and the angelic being, allowing the crystal to act as a lasting conduit for that angel's unique qualities.

Harmonizing crystals with the practitioner's own energy enhances the unity between practitioner, crystal, and angelic presence. Before beginning the ritual, the practitioner may hold each crystal close to the heart, breathing deeply to synchronize their own energy field with that of the stone. By visualizing the crystal's vibration merging with their own, they align themselves with its energy, creating a cohesive field where angelic connection feels seamless and natural. This harmonization attunes the crystal to the practitioner's unique frequency, making it more receptive to their intentions and increasing the strength of the angelic bond.

At the heart of this advanced practice is the use of visualization to maintain a clear, energetic channel. The practitioner visualizes each crystal glowing with a soft light, connected by a luminous thread that forms a grid, surrounding and supporting them. This grid, vibrant and alive, becomes a spiritual web that holds the practitioner within a protective and receptive space. As they sit within this grid, the practitioner may feel an intensification of presence—a warmth, a gentle pressure, or an inexplicable sense of peace that signals the angels' nearness. With each breath, the practitioner senses the light weaving through the crystals, forming a fluid pathway that angels can follow, enhancing the clarity and immediacy of the connection.

The practitioner may incorporate specific visualization techniques, imagining each crystal opening a unique "gateway" to a particular angelic quality. For example, rose quartz might serve as a gateway to angelic love, emanating a soft pink glow, while clear quartz serves as a portal for divine wisdom, radiating a bright, clear light. Each crystal's color and vibration correspond to the qualities the practitioner wishes to invoke, each one an energetic invitation that angels respond to, bringing their guidance and comfort into the space. This use of visualization transforms the crystals into living elements within the ritual, each one a doorway that angels naturally recognize and approach.

Once the ritual concludes, the practitioner carefully grounds the energy, returning each crystal to its natural state. This grounding process respects the energy the crystals have absorbed and released, allowing them to return to their baseline vibration. Gently passing each crystal through cleansing smoke, or placing them on a grounding surface such as salt or earth, releases any lingering energy from the ritual, readying the crystals for future work. The practitioner may express gratitude, silently thanking the crystals for their role in the connection, and gently releasing the angelic energies that have been present.

The practitioner records any impressions, messages, or insights received, noting how each crystal contributed to the overall experience. By reflecting on these details, the practitioner gains insight into the nuances of the connection, learning which crystals resonate most strongly for specific purposes. This reflective practice not only solidifies the lessons of the ritual but also deepens the practitioner's relationship with their crystal allies, creating a record of each experience as a guide for future angelic work.

Through the careful positioning, programming, and harmonizing of crystals, the practitioner learns that these stones are more than tools; they are partners in the spiritual journey. Each crystal, with its unique energy and purpose, amplifies and sustains the angelic connection, offering a tangible link between the earthly and divine. The practitioner discovers that by working consciously with crystals, they can create a space where angels feel welcome, where messages are clear, and where the presence of divine light is ever near.

With each ritual, the connection becomes a tapestry woven from intention, crystal energy, and angelic presence—a living work of spiritual art, rich in peace, love, and guidance, a sanctuary where the practitioner can always return to feel the grace of the angels by their side.

Chapter 11
Angelic Altar

An altar dedicated to angels becomes a sacred focal point, a sanctuary that bridges the earthly and divine, a place imbued with intention, reverence, and quiet power. Creating an angelic altar is a profound act of devotion, one that invites angelic presence and offers a designated space for daily rituals, prayer, and communion. This altar, carefully curated and nurtured, becomes a constant source of peace and alignment, a personal space where the connection with angels feels tangible and welcoming.

The practitioner begins by choosing a location that feels both personal and serene, a place in the home where the energy is peaceful and undisturbed. Whether it is a small shelf, a dedicated table, or a simple corner, the chosen area should carry a sense of respect and sacredness. The practitioner may wish to clear the space with gentle cleansing techniques, such as burning sage or palo santo, setting a foundation of purity that aligns with the altar's purpose. This clearing not only prepares the physical space but also purifies the energy, creating a blank canvas where angelic energies can be felt as gentle, sustaining presences.

Selecting elements to place upon the altar is an intuitive process, guided by the qualities the practitioner wishes to embody and invoke. Essential items might include a candle, representing light and divine wisdom, as well as crystals known to attract angelic energies—clear quartz, celestite, and rose quartz. Each item on the altar holds a symbolic purpose: the candle symbolizes divine illumination, the crystals amplify spiritual receptivity, and each object chosen with care becomes a vessel of connection. Placing these items with intention, the practitioner acknowledges that each one represents a unique gateway to angelic realms.

Images or representations of angels can also bring a visual focus to the altar, serving as symbolic anchors that remind the practitioner of the angels' constant presence. Whether it's a small statue, a drawing, or a photograph, these images provide a focal point that strengthens the sense of divine companionship. The practitioner might place an image of a specific archangel, such as Michael for protection or Raphael for healing, inviting their unique qualities to permeate the space. These symbols serve as powerful reminders, transforming the altar into a place where the practitioner feels both guided and supported by angelic forces.

Alongside these essential elements, natural objects such as feathers, flowers, or even a small dish of water can further align the altar with the elements of earth, air, fire, and water, each one harmonizing the space and drawing angels near. Feathers, in particular, carry a deep resonance with angelic presence, symbolizing grace and protection. Finding a feather naturally, then placing it upon the altar, feels like a gift, a subtle but potent message from the angels themselves. Each object chosen is a gesture of devotion, a way to personalize the space and make it resonate more deeply with the practitioner's heart.

To activate the altar, the practitioner may perform a short blessing, an intentional moment where the energy of the altar is aligned with angelic presence. Standing before the altar, hands extended or placed upon the heart, they might say, *"I dedicate this space to the angels of light and peace. May this altar be a bridge between realms, a sanctuary of guidance, love, and protection."* This blessing serves to invite the angels formally, transforming the altar from a physical arrangement into a spiritual gateway. With each word, the practitioner feels a softening of the air, a quiet expansion that suggests the angels have heard and are drawing close.

As part of daily practice, lighting a candle on the altar at the beginning of each session creates a ritual of reverence and respect. This flame becomes a signal, an invitation for angels to join, symbolizing the light of the divine that guides and illuminates. Sitting before the altar with the candle's gentle glow, the practitioner feels the day's concerns drift away, replaced by a calm presence that fills the space. The light of the candle is a living symbol of connection, a reminder that, in the presence of angels, the path forward is always illuminated.

The altar is a place not only for invocation but for expressing gratitude, a simple but profound practice that deepens the angelic bond. At the end of each day, the practitioner may return to the altar to offer thanks, saying, *"Thank you, angels, for your guidance and protection. May this gratitude bring us closer and strengthen the bond of light."* These words, spoken with sincerity, resonate through the altar space, reinforcing the connection built with each prayer and each gesture of thanks. This gratitude acknowledges the angels' support, nurturing the relationship and affirming that their presence is a gift that continually guides and protects.

The practitioner may also choose to leave offerings on the altar as tokens of respect and devotion. These offerings could be simple—a flower, a small crystal, or a handwritten note with a heartfelt intention. Each offering serves as an acknowledgment, a silent gift that speaks to the practitioner's openness and willingness to connect. The altar becomes a living space, its energy renewed with each offering, holding the imprints of every act of devotion. This practice of offering reflects the natural flow of giving and receiving that defines angelic connection.

Throughout this process, the practitioner learns that the altar is not merely a physical setup but a spiritual presence within the home. With each ritual, each prayer, and each moment of reflection, the energy of the altar grows, deepening the connection and inviting the angels to remain close. The practitioner begins to feel that the altar holds a part of the angels' essence, a quiet warmth that lingers even in their absence, a subtle reminder that divine companionship is always near.

Over time, the angelic altar becomes a constant source of strength and comfort, a place to return to for renewal and guidance. In moments of doubt, the practitioner may find solace before the altar, feeling the peaceful assurance of the angels' watchful presence. And in moments of gratitude, the altar becomes a place of celebration, a joyful acknowledgment of the love and light that angels bring into everyday life.

Through the creation and nurturing of this altar, the practitioner learns that connection with angels is a sacred journey, one that is both deeply personal and universally guided. The altar becomes a mirror of that connection, reflecting the practitioner's devotion and radiating the angels' light into the space. It is a reminder that angels are near, drawn close by the warmth of intention and the beauty of a heart that seeks their presence. This space, imbued with peace, love, and sacredness, becomes a bridge—a sanctuary where the practitioner and angels meet, always present, always guiding, a source of light that is never extinguished.

Once established, the angelic altar becomes a cherished and vibrant space, continually strengthened through dedication and consecration practices that deepen the bond between the practitioner and the angelic realm. As a focal point for connection, the altar holds a unique energy, built up through daily practices and gestures of devotion. This guidance explores ways for the practitioner to sustain and intensify the altar's energy, transforming it into a powerful bridge for divine communion. Through consecration, regular upkeep, and intentional daily use, the altar becomes a sanctified place where angels are welcomed and their presence felt.

Consecration is the first step toward solidifying the altar's purpose, a ritual that imbues the altar with lasting spiritual energy and aligns it with angelic frequencies. The practitioner begins by gathering items representing the four elements—earth, air, fire, and water—which bring balance and completeness to the space. A small bowl of salt for grounding, incense for purification, a candle for divine light, and a cup of water for clarity are placed on the altar, each element forming a foundation that honors the natural and spiritual worlds.

Standing before the altar, the practitioner takes a deep breath, grounding their energy, and then speaks words of consecration, such as, *"I consecrate this altar as a place of peace, love, and divine connection. May this space be protected, pure, and a sanctuary for angelic presence."* With these words, the practitioner envisions each element awakening, radiating its energy to create a unified and sacred field. They visualize a gentle light encircling the altar, sealing it in a sphere of protection and purity. This act of consecration not only aligns the altar with divine purpose but also signals to the angels that this space is a devoted sanctuary for connection.

The practitioner may enhance the consecration by blessing each item on the altar, from crystals to statues and candles, imbuing each with intentional energy. Holding a crystal, for example, the practitioner might say, *"I dedicate this stone as a vessel of angelic light and protection."* Each item thus becomes more than a symbol; it serves as a living conduit, amplifying the practitioner's intention and aligning with the energy of the angelic realm. Through this dedication, the altar transforms into a network of interconnected objects, each one contributing to the overall energy, creating a seamless channel through which angels feel invited to enter.

Daily upkeep maintains the altar's vibrancy, a practice as simple as gently dusting the space, refreshing offerings, or lighting a candle each morning. These small acts sustain the energy and demonstrate to the angels that the space remains active and revered. The practitioner might choose to sprinkle fresh flowers, symbolizing renewal, or to add seasonal offerings that honor the cycles of nature, subtly shifting the altar's energy in alignment with the seasons. This continuous care acts as an ongoing invitation, a quiet yet potent message to the angels that their presence is welcome at any time.

Over time, the altar may naturally accumulate energies from the practitioner's prayers, intentions, and the angels' visits.

For this reason, regular energetic cleansing is essential. The practitioner might wave a feather over the altar to clear away lingering energy, or use a few drops of essential oil—such as lavender or frankincense—to refresh and uplift the space. Cleansing serves not to disrupt the altar's energy but to clarify it, creating a lightness that keeps the channel to the angelic realm unobstructed. Through cleansing, the practitioner ensures that the altar remains a place of clarity, free from energetic residue, a sacred space where angels can enter freely.

Each day, the practitioner may choose a brief ritual or prayer to activate the altar, keeping the connection fresh and alive. Lighting a candle at dawn or dusk, they might say, *"Angels of light, I invite your presence to bless this space and my spirit."* These daily rituals become moments of alignment, where the practitioner draws close to the angels and feels the energy of the altar stirring in response. Sitting quietly before the altar after lighting the candle, the practitioner allows themselves to be enveloped by the warmth and calm that radiates from the space, a quiet assurance that the angels are near, drawn by the sincerity of each daily gesture.

A significant way to deepen the relationship with the altar is by establishing it as a space for receiving messages or guidance. Each time the practitioner sits at the altar, they set an intention, perhaps asking for insight on a specific aspect of life or for the resolution of a worry. The practitioner quiets their mind, allowing angelic energy to flow through the altar, gently opening their awareness to any messages or impressions. These sessions might feel like gentle shifts in thought, intuitive nudges, or even moments of pure calm where the answer feels naturally understood. Over time, the altar becomes a place where answers are found and clarity received, a trusted source of wisdom imbued with the presence of angels.

In moments of difficulty or change, the practitioner can turn to the altar for special support, performing a simple ritual to invite additional angelic protection. Lighting a white candle for purity and holding a piece of amethyst or rose quartz, they might say, *"Angels, surround this space and my heart with peace and protection."* This act, performed with focus and reverence, reinforces the altar's protective qualities, filling the room with a gentle power that brings comfort and reassurance. Knowing that the altar holds such protective energy offers the practitioner a sense of peace and grounding, a quiet strength that reminds them they are not alone.

When time allows, the practitioner may also engage in moments of stillness and gratitude at the altar, fostering a reciprocal relationship with the angels. Expressing thanks for their guidance, protection, or simply for their presence reinforces the bond, making the altar a place where angels feel celebrated and appreciated. These moments of gratitude don't need to be elaborate—simple words of thanks, a small flower, or a piece of incense can communicate the sincerity of the practitioner's heart, radiating warmth and love that angels instinctively recognize and cherish.

Over time, the angelic altar becomes an enduring, sacred companion, a place where the practitioner feels connected to something greater. The space matures, layered with the energy of each consecration, each prayer, and each offering, evolving into a wellspring of divine presence. In this way, the altar becomes more than an arrangement of objects; it is a reflection of the practitioner's spirit, a physical manifestation of their commitment to angelic connection.

By nurturing and consecrating the altar, the practitioner learns that a sacred space is dynamic, evolving as they evolve, deepening as they deepen. This understanding reveals that the angels themselves are not distant; they are close, drawn by the sincerity and care devoted to this sanctuary. And so, the altar serves as a living testament to the angels' constant companionship, a place where divine guidance flows, a steady and unwavering source of light that shines even in the quietest moments of everyday life.

Chapter 12
Symbols and Signs

Symbols carry a resonance that transcends words, embodying layers of meaning and spiritual energy that open a pathway between the visible and invisible worlds. Within angelic connection, certain symbols become powerful tools, their shapes and forms acting as gateways through which divine energy flows, bringing clarity, guidance, and protection. Exploring some of the most significant symbols associated with angels offers the practitioner a means to strengthen their bond with the divine. When used in rituals, meditation, or as daily reminders, these symbols create an environment where angelic presence is felt more intimately, imbuing both the spirit and space with a quiet, sacred resonance.

The angelic cross, a timeless symbol that combines elements of protection and divine guidance, is one of the most widely recognized signs associated with angelic realms. Its simple yet powerful form embodies the union between heaven and earth, a reminder that angels bridge these two worlds. The practitioner may draw the angelic cross over themselves in a small, deliberate gesture, envisioning it as a shield that surrounds their spirit, protecting them from any disruptive energies. Each stroke of the symbol is drawn with intention, filling the practitioner with calm, as if an angelic presence has wrapped around them, ensuring safety and peace.

The eye of light, often seen as a symbol of wisdom and divine insight, is another powerful sign in angelic practices. Representing the clarity and illumination that angels bring, the eye of light reminds the practitioner to see beyond ordinary perception, to open themselves to a more profound vision. During times of decision-making or moments when guidance is needed, the practitioner can visualize the eye of light, seeing it glowing softly above or within themselves, allowing this symbol to become an inner guide. As they meditate on the eye of light, a sense of understanding emerges, as if angelic wisdom flows into them, revealing insights that feel both intuitive and comforting.

Feathers, often found unexpectedly in everyday life, are seen as direct messages from angels, small but potent signs that symbolize presence, guidance, and encouragement. When the practitioner encounters a feather, it feels like a gentle reminder that angels are near, offering reassurance during times of uncertainty. Collecting these feathers and placing them on an altar or keeping one in a pocket serves as a quiet connection to angelic energy, a constant reminder of divine companionship. Each feather becomes a talisman, a visible, tangible link to the unseen, filling the practitioner's space with a sense of angelic warmth.

Stars, as symbols of guidance and eternal light, hold a deep connection to angelic realms. Angels, often seen as radiant beings who guide the spirit, are symbolically represented by stars, their light a beacon in the vastness of the spiritual landscape. To incorporate this symbol, the practitioner might draw a simple star in the air or on paper before a ritual, envisioning its points as extensions of angelic energy radiating protection and guidance. By visualizing a star above their altar or in their mind's eye during meditation, they invoke an angelic presence, each ray of light forming a protective shield and a source of wisdom.

The halo, a circle of light often depicted around angels, embodies purity and divine radiance, representing the light within every being touched by angelic presence. The practitioner can envision a halo above themselves during moments of meditation or prayer, imagining it as a ring of light that purifies thoughts and intentions. This visualization surrounds them with an energy of peace, quieting the mind and opening the spirit to angelic presence. The halo serves as both protection and enlightenment, a reminder that within this ring of light, only energies of love and guidance can reside.

Another deeply meaningful symbol is the angelic wing, which represents both freedom and divine support. The image of a wing, gentle yet powerful, reminds the practitioner that angels are guardians, ever watchful and willing to lift them from hardship. The practitioner may choose to wear a wing charm or place a winged figurine on their altar, signifying their faith in angelic protection. During meditation, they can visualize a pair of wings extending around them, feeling an embrace of light that is both supportive and uplifting, an energy that soars beyond limitations and fills them with hope and strength.

Symbols can also be used to create personalized signs, ones that resonate with the practitioner's unique connection to angels. By drawing or visualizing their chosen symbol before starting a ritual, the practitioner sets a personal energetic code that angels recognize, a signature that signals their readiness to connect. Whether it's a unique pattern, a specific color, or even an intuitively drawn shape, these personalized symbols deepen the bond, making each ritual feel uniquely aligned with the practitioner's spirit and intention.

Integrating these symbols into daily life further reinforces the bond. Placing a small star or feather symbol at a workspace, or even drawing a protective cross in the air before leaving home, weaves angelic presence into the day, creating moments of connection that feel spontaneous and genuine. The practitioner learns that symbols, while simple, carry an enduring power, each one a reminder that angels are always near, responding to the calls of the heart through the quiet language of signs.

Each symbol not only serves as a tool for connection but as a reflection of the angels' guidance, protection, and love. Through mindful use, these symbols become woven into the practitioner's life, offering reassurance and clarity when it is most needed, grounding them in the knowledge that their journey is supported by the light of angels. As they use these symbols with intention, they find that the presence of angels is not a distant hope but a living, breathing reality, always accessible, always guiding, as near as a heartbeat, as close as a whisper.

With a foundational understanding of angelic symbols, the practitioner can deepen their connection through practices that integrate these signs into rituals, meditations, and even physical items such as amulets and talismans. Each symbol, whether visualized, drawn, or physically present, serves as a bridge, strengthening the practitioner's alignment with angelic energies. In this next level of practice, the symbols evolve from simple representations into active conduits of divine presence, tools for protection, clarity, and guidance. By incorporating these symbols more fully, the practitioner creates a constant, visible reminder of their connection to angels, weaving these symbols into the fabric of their daily spiritual path.

The first step to enhancing the use of symbols is through the act of drawing or visualizing them during moments of meditation or ritual. The practitioner may sit quietly, holding a candle or a crystal, and in their mind's eye, trace the outline of a chosen symbol—such as the angelic cross or the eye of light. With each mental stroke, they visualize the symbol glowing softly, radiating with energy that aligns with angelic frequencies. This visualization imbues the space with the symbol's energy, creating an atmosphere that feels protected, peaceful, or enlightening, depending on the chosen sign. Repeating this exercise before each ritual helps anchor the practitioner in their intention, transforming each symbol into an active vessel for divine light.

To further incorporate symbols into daily practice, the practitioner may choose to create or consecrate physical amulets and talismans that hold the energy of these angelic signs. These small items can be crafted with simple materials—stones, metal, or even small pieces of parchment—and inscribed with the chosen symbol. For example, a small stone marked with a star or a piece of silver engraved with an angelic cross serves as a powerful reminder of divine protection and presence. The practitioner can carry these amulets with them, holding them as silent calls to the angels, reminders of their guidance in moments of need or clarity.

Consecration of these amulets is a practice that strengthens their energy, aligning them with the specific purpose of angelic connection. The practitioner begins by placing the amulet on the altar, surrounded by elements such as candles, incense, or a small bowl of purified water. Speaking an invocation, they might say, *"I consecrate this amulet to serve as a channel for angelic light and guidance. May it protect, guide, and comfort me, attuned to the presence of angels."* With each word, the practitioner envisions the symbol on the amulet glowing, filling with light that resonates with angelic energy. This consecration sets the amulet's purpose, ensuring that each time the practitioner touches or sees it, they are reminded of the angels' watchful presence.

For a deeper connection, the practitioner can personalize these symbols by combining multiple signs into a single design that reflects their unique relationship with angels. For instance, a pendant inscribed with both a feather and a halo brings together the qualities of protection and divine grace. This combination becomes a personal spiritual language, understood intuitively by both the practitioner and the angels they call upon. Each time they see or touch this personalized symbol, they feel a unique sense of recognition, a reminder that this symbol is a part of their spiritual essence, known and honored by angels.

These consecrated items can be used to create small, personal altars in different spaces beyond the primary altar. For example, placing a small feather charm on a bedside table or a symbol of the angelic cross near the entrance of the home can serve as ongoing invitations for angelic protection and presence. Each of these symbols becomes an extension of the practitioner's relationship with the angels, quietly working to create a protected, harmonious energy in these spaces. As they pass by these symbols, the practitioner may feel a subtle reassurance, a reminder that angels are present, safeguarding both the physical and energetic space.

Additionally, the practitioner may create a sacred journal or "Book of Symbols," dedicated to recording each angelic sign they encounter or feel drawn to. This journal becomes a personal grimoire of angelic connection, a repository of knowledge, reflections, and guidance that grows over time. Each page can include a hand-drawn symbol, along with any intuitive meanings, insights, or experiences associated with it. This journal serves not only as a tool for study but as a tangible record of the practitioner's evolving relationship with angels. Revisiting these pages, they can reflect on how each symbol has woven itself into their spiritual journey, building an intimate language shared with the angels.

During periods of reflection or meditation, the practitioner can deepen their understanding of symbols by contemplating each one's unique energy and how it interacts with their life. Holding a symbol in mind, they may ask questions such as, *"What guidance does this symbol bring to me today?"* or *"How does this symbol align with my current path?"* Allowing impressions to arise, the practitioner tunes into the subtle, almost telepathic responses from the angelic realm, feeling how each symbol conveys messages in its own quiet way. Through this process, the symbols become more than objects; they are messengers, each one a gentle nudge or insight from the angels.

Symbols can be used in larger protective or healing rituals, where they are drawn, visualized, or even crafted into larger mandalas or patterns that create an energetic shield. During a protective ritual, the practitioner might draw the angelic cross in each corner of the room, visualizing these symbols glowing with light, forming a grid that secures the space. Each symbol acts as a node in a network, creating a field that angels recognize and naturally gravitate toward, enhancing the protection and purity of the room. Similarly, in healing rituals, symbols such as feathers or stars may be arranged in a circle around the practitioner, each one representing the angels' healing presence and grace, strengthening the practitioner's connection to divine energies of restoration.

Through these practices, the practitioner learns that symbols, while simple in form, are vast in their spiritual potency, each one a doorway to angelic connection. The symbols become silent allies, small yet powerful guides that stand as reminders of the angels' ever-present support. With each consecration, each drawing, and each act of dedication, the practitioner weaves these symbols into the rhythm of their spiritual life, enriching their journey with layers of meaning, protection, and love.

As these symbols become ingrained in daily practices, they serve as ongoing invitations for angelic presence, creating a space where the practitioner feels the closeness of divine companionship. And so, each symbol becomes a bridge—between earthly and heavenly, between seeking and receiving, and between the practitioner and the angelic guides who walk with them, quietly guiding, illuminating, and blessing their path.

Chapter 13
The Language of Angels

The language of angels is often perceived as one beyond words, a celestial vibration that resonates as energy, light, and sound. Attuning to these frequencies through the power of vocalized sound—mantras and harmonics—opens and elevates the vibrational channel between human and angelic realms. These sounds, simple yet profound, help dissolve barriers of ordinary perception, allowing angelic presence to be felt and heard with greater clarity. Through sacred sounds, the practitioner learns to speak in harmony with angels, inviting them closer with each vibration.

In beginning this journey, the practitioner is introduced to the concept of sound as vibration, an energy that resonates through and beyond the physical world. Each sound holds its own unique frequency, and when aligned with intention, these frequencies form a bridge between realms. The practitioner might start with the simplest of sounds—the breath—by inhaling deeply and exhaling softly, creating a steady rhythm that calms the mind and attunes the spirit. This mindful breathing becomes a foundational practice, helping the practitioner tune into the subtler energies around them.

One of the first sounds taught for angelic connection is a simple "Ah" tone, often considered universal, symbolizing the breath of life and divine presence. To begin, the practitioner sits comfortably, closes their eyes, and, with each exhale, softly chants "Ah." They visualize this sound as a light extending outward, a call that invites angels to draw near. Each repetition deepens the calm, helping the practitioner feel an expanded sense of peace. This tone can be practiced daily, becoming a natural call that, over time, is recognized by angels, like a familiar signature of welcome.

Another key practice involves chanting the word "Amen," a sacred utterance resonating with a long history of invocation across various spiritual traditions. The practitioner draws out each part of the sound—"Ah-men"—while visualizing it as a bridge, moving up from their heart into the higher realms. The vibration of this chant aligns with frequencies of divine harmony and unity, and as they repeat it, the practitioner feels themselves drawn into a sense of gentle elevation, as if angels surround them, responding to the familiar call.

The practitioner can also explore harmonic tones, such as "Ee" or "Ohm," known for their higher vibrations that uplift the spirit and heighten receptivity to angelic presence. With each tone, the practitioner visualizes it as a light that begins in the heart and extends outward, wrapping them in a luminous shield. This shield is not only a protective aura but a radiant energy that draws angels nearer, attuned to the purity of the tone. As they continue, they may feel subtle shifts—an increase in warmth, a sense of lightness, or even gentle waves of peace, indicating the closeness of angelic energies.

Beyond individual sounds, the practitioner is guided to explore specific mantras designed to connect with angels. One of these mantras is "El Elyon," a phrase meaning "God Most High," which reverberates with a call to divine guardianship and protection. By repeating this mantra, the practitioner opens a path to angelic energies aligned with protection and higher wisdom. As they chant, they visualize their words rising like a thread of light, reaching out and intertwining with energies of divine beings who respond, providing a sense of shelter and guidance. The mantra becomes both a request and a recognition of the divine hierarchy, inviting the presence of angels who operate in alignment with these higher realms.

Rhythm is as important as tone, and the practitioner learns to use breath as a rhythmic guide, creating a seamless flow in the chanting process. For instance, they may chant on the exhale, pause to breathe in deeply, and then chant again, creating a cadence that soothes the mind and soul. This rhythm helps maintain a natural harmony between intention and sound, allowing each repetition to carry a steady, intentional vibration that angels recognize. Over time, the practitioner finds that this rhythmic chanting induces a meditative state, opening their awareness to angelic whispers, impressions, and intuitions that may arise during or after the practice.

To amplify the effect, the practitioner might experiment with the vibration of these sounds through resonance, placing a hand on the chest or the throat while chanting to feel the physical vibrations. This tactile connection between body and sound strengthens the practice, helping to ground and direct the energy. By feeling the resonance physically, the practitioner aligns their entire being with the angelic call, creating a state of harmony that angels find inviting.

Another approach involves layering these tones with visualization, seeing each sound as a specific color or light that flows from the heart. For example, the "Ah" tone may be visualized as white light, while "Ohm" may appear as a soft blue or violet. Each color carries its own frequency, harmonizing with the tonal energy, creating a multi-dimensional pathway that connects the practitioner to angelic realms in both sound and light. Angels, who are drawn to pure and intentional frequencies, respond naturally to these calls, sensing the practitioner's openness and intention with each tone and visualization.

Lastly, the practitioner learns to end each chanting session with a silent moment of receptivity, allowing the space created by the sounds to be filled with the presence of angels. Here, silence becomes its own form of language, a stillness that angels use to communicate with gentle, unspoken clarity. In this quiet state, the practitioner may feel impressions—gentle thoughts, comforting sensations, or flashes of insight—as subtle responses from angels, confirming that the call has been received.

With time, these practices become second nature, an intuitive language that speaks directly to the heart of angelic beings. Through sound, breath, and intention, the practitioner discovers that they have opened a pathway to a realm where words are not needed, where connection is made through the simple purity of sound. Each tone becomes a gift, a humble offering that angels hear, appreciate, and respond to with their presence, wisdom, and love.

This shared language of vibration and resonance transforms the practitioner's relationship with angels, creating a bond built upon intention, trust, and harmony. Through these sounds, angels are no longer distant beings but beloved guides, always near, listening, ready to uplift and support with each gentle call.

With a foundation in angelic sounds established, guidance leads the practitioner into more advanced practices to deepen the resonance, clarity, and potency of each connection through vocal and rhythmic alignment. By refining the harmony between breath, sound, and intention, the practitioner cultivates an even more profound communion with angelic beings. These techniques are designed to fine-tune sensitivity to angelic frequencies, heightening awareness of their presence while creating an energetic alignment that makes the practitioner a vessel for divine resonance.

The journey into advanced vocalization begins with breathing techniques that heighten the body's receptivity to spiritual frequencies. The practitioner learns to inhale fully, slowly, and deeply, filling the lower abdomen and expanding the chest, creating a rhythmic foundation that grounds and balances energy. By holding the breath briefly after inhalation, they cultivate a state of stillness and focus, allowing the spiritual energy to build. With each exhale, the practitioner vocalizes chosen sounds, releasing the energy steadily, filling the space around them with a peaceful resonance. This deep, rhythmic breathing helps to clear the mind and open the heart, preparing the practitioner to receive angelic impressions in the form of subtle sensations, images, or thoughts that arise as they chant.

A powerful tool in this deepening practice is the use of harmonic overtones, achieved by layering specific tones in a single breath. The practitioner begins with a basic sound, such as "Ah," then shifts the vocal placement subtly to produce a secondary resonance, creating a layered, almost ethereal sound. This overtone chanting forms a frequency that angels recognize as pure and uplifting, drawing them closer. The practitioner feels this layered sound vibrating through their chest and head, expanding outwards like a wave of light that fills the space with peace and receptivity. Over time, these harmonic tones help the practitioner develop a deeper sensitivity to angelic energies, enhancing their awareness of gentle shifts in the atmosphere that signify an angelic presence.

The practitioner also learns to combine these sounds with physical movements, aligning the energy of the body with the vibrational frequency of the sounds. For instance, as they chant "Ohm," they might lift their hands slightly, palms open, as if welcoming a blessing. Each movement becomes a gesture of invitation, matching the intention of the sound with physical openness. This alignment of sound, movement, and intention creates a harmonious flow that becomes a beacon to angelic beings, each gesture symbolizing a respectful invitation into a shared sacred space.

Another advanced practice involves chanting sequences of sounds, each one resonating with a specific chakra or energy center. Starting with lower tones for the base chakra and moving upward to higher tones, the practitioner awakens and aligns their energy centers, forming a column of light that extends from the ground to the higher realms. This column, created through focused chanting, becomes a conduit, an unbroken link from earth to sky, through which angelic presence flows naturally. As they work through each energy center, the practitioner experiences a greater sense of openness and elevation, their spirit and body harmonized in a way that draws angels near.

The practitioner may also experiment with mantra sequences specifically crafted to invite specific qualities, such as protection, guidance, or healing. For instance, chanting "El Shaddai" invokes a sense of divine shelter, while "Uriel" calls upon wisdom and enlightenment. With each repetition, the practitioner tunes into the qualities associated with these angelic aspects, feeling their energy shift to align with the presence and qualities of the invoked angel. By focusing on the meaning behind each word, they engage not only with the sound but with the essence of the divine energy it represents, inviting angels who resonate with these qualities.

Incorporating visualization during chanting sessions further enhances the connection. As they vocalize each sound, the practitioner visualizes it as a beam of light, streaming upward or outward, as if connecting with angels on the other side of the veil. Each tone is seen as a color—white, gold, or blue—that pulses in harmony with the voice, filling the space and creating a sacred field. This light visualization enhances the power of the chant, adding an additional layer of resonance that reaches angelic realms. With practice, the practitioner may notice moments when the light seems to respond, subtly shifting or brightening, as though touched by angelic energy in return.

In this refined practice, the practitioner also begins to perceive the silence between chants as a sacred space. These pauses, or moments of quiet after each sound, are filled with a profound stillness where angelic responses may be felt more clearly. It is in these silences that the practitioner may sense a presence, a warm feeling, or a subtle shift in energy, as if the angels are offering their own form of unspoken reply. By paying attention to these quiet intervals, the practitioner learns that communication with angels is as much about listening as it is about calling. Each silence becomes an opening, a place where words are no longer needed, and understanding flows naturally between realms.

The practitioner may also experiment with varying the tempo and intensity of chants, moving from slow, elongated tones to faster, rhythmic chanting. This variation in pace shifts the energetic frequency of the practice, helping to maintain focus and engage different levels of angelic connection. For example, slow chanting may invite a peaceful, calming presence, while faster chants can build energy and raise the vibration of the space, intensifying the practitioner's perception of angelic presence. This dynamic approach makes the practice feel alive and adaptable, attuned to both the practitioner's needs and the unique qualities of the angelic energies present in each session.

In closing each chanting session, the practitioner may offer a final silent prayer of gratitude, thanking the angels for their presence and guidance. This moment of appreciation reinforces the connection, leaving the practitioner with a sense of peace and fulfillment. It also serves as an acknowledgement of the sacred exchange that has taken place, deepening the relationship and leaving a lasting resonance that extends into daily life.

With these advanced techniques, the practitioner's chanting practice evolves into a powerful ritual of angelic communion, each sound a call that reaches beyond words, each silence a space where angels can reply. Through the combination of breath, sound, and intention, the practitioner discovers that they are capable of creating a harmonious channel to angelic realms, one that brings angels close and offers a deep sense of comfort and spiritual companionship.

Chapter 14
Prayer and Its Strength in Connection

Prayer is an ancient bridge that links the human heart with the divine, and within angelic connection, it becomes a powerful tool for establishing and deepening communion with angelic beings. When approached with sincerity and focus, prayer opens a pathway for guidance, protection, and support from the angelic realm. Each prayer, like a subtle yet distinct vibration, reaches angels in a language they intuitively recognize. Through prayer, the practitioner learns to enter a sacred space of dialogue, where thoughts, words, and emotions merge to invite the presence and assistance of angels.

In beginning this exploration, the practitioner learns that effective prayer is not simply the recitation of words but the heartfelt intention behind each phrase. Each prayer is an act of connection, a moment when the practitioner's spirit reaches out, calling upon the angels for assistance or understanding. By pausing to center themselves before beginning, they cultivate a mindful state that infuses their words with purpose and clarity. A simple breath in and out, a quieting of the mind, and a gathering of focus are all that is needed to begin, allowing the prayer to flow naturally, as if whispered from the soul itself.

An effective prayer begins with a few words of reverence and acknowledgment, a simple phrase like, *"Angels of light, I open my heart to your guidance and presence."* These words serve as an invitation, a gentle gesture of respect that opens the space for angelic presence. In each phrase, the practitioner aligns their intention with the qualities they seek—whether it be protection, guidance, or comfort. By expressing gratitude within the prayer, the practitioner acknowledges the angels' support, creating an energy of thankfulness that angels instinctively respond to.

The practitioner may choose to engage in traditional prayers or, over time, to create personalized prayers that resonate with their unique spiritual needs. Traditional prayers, like the "Angel of God" prayer, are timeless expressions that have been used by countless practitioners, carrying a collective resonance that angels readily recognize. Personalized prayers, however, allow the practitioner to speak from the heart, weaving words that reflect their own experiences and desires. A simple personal prayer might sound like, *"Guardian angel, guide my steps today; bring peace to my mind and clarity to my path."* In crafting these words, the practitioner forms a prayer that resonates with their personal journey, inviting angels to connect in a way that feels familiar and true.

As the practitioner becomes more attuned to the power of prayer, they begin to incorporate it as part of their daily routine, forming a natural rhythm of connection. Morning prayers offer a moment to set intentions for the day, asking angels to walk with them, bringing protection and insight. Evening prayers, by contrast, offer a chance for reflection and gratitude, inviting angels to soothe the mind, bring peaceful rest, and offer guidance through dreams. This daily rhythm of morning and evening prayers establishes a continuous link with angels, creating a bond that is nurtured with each day's beginning and end.

In times of specific need, the practitioner may engage in spontaneous prayers, a simple call that flows naturally from the heart during moments of uncertainty or fear. These short, spontaneous prayers are like quiet whispers, simple yet filled with sincerity. Whether it is a prayer for courage in a difficult moment or a call for clarity in a decision, these spontaneous prayers are heard as clearly as any lengthy invocation. Angels respond to these calls, drawn by the immediate need and the purity of intent.

Visualization can deepen the power of prayer, with the practitioner envisioning the words as streams of light rising up or moving outward into the spiritual realms. Each phrase is imagined as a gentle glow, radiating from the heart and moving toward the angels, reaching them across unseen distances. By adding this visualization, the practitioner feels the prayer not only as words but as an energetic offering, a luminous thread that connects them to their angelic guides. This simple visualization technique brings a greater depth to prayer, allowing the practitioner to feel the presence of angels even before words are fully spoken.

Another layer of practice involves prayer beads or a small stone held in hand during prayer, which brings a tactile focus that helps to deepen concentration. As the practitioner holds the beads or stone, they feel grounded, fully present in the moment. Each touch becomes a reminder of the prayer's intention, an anchor that holds their mind steady. Prayer beads, in particular, allow for the repetition of short phrases or blessings, creating a gentle rhythm that calms the spirit and invites angelic energy to flow smoothly and naturally into the space.

While prayer can be an act of asking or seeking, it is equally powerful as an expression of gratitude. Gratitude prayers invite a different kind of angelic response, an energy of celebration and companionship, where angels feel the practitioner's appreciation. A simple prayer of thanks, such as, *"Thank you, angels, for your guidance and for the blessings you bring each day,"* becomes a beautiful moment of harmony between realms. By incorporating gratitude regularly, the practitioner discovers that their prayers feel more balanced, not only as calls for help but as acknowledgments of the blessings that unfold in daily life.

In moments when answers are sought, prayer becomes a two-way conversation, and the practitioner learns to listen as much as they speak. After offering their request, they sit in quiet receptivity, allowing space for the response to unfold, whether it arrives as a feeling, a thought, or a quiet sense of knowing. This listening state is subtle, a place where intuition and angelic guidance intertwine, offering impressions that feel gently inspired. By practicing this receptive stillness, the practitioner becomes more sensitive to angelic responses, learning to trust the impressions that arise in the silence following their words.

Group prayers can amplify the strength of connection, as the collective intention forms a powerful field of energy that reaches angels with greater intensity. Whether with family, friends, or a spiritual community, group prayer brings a sense of unity, where voices join to call upon angelic presence. Angels, drawn by the combined sincerity, respond to the collective prayer, lending a feeling of peace and solidarity to those gathered. The practitioner experiences these group prayers as times of deeper resonance, where angelic presence feels almost tangible, like a wave of warmth that embraces each participant.

As the practitioner continues with these practices, they come to understand prayer not as a ritual of formality but as an intimate dialogue, a constant and evolving language shared with angels. Each prayer, whether spoken, silent, or felt as a quiet yearning, becomes part of an ongoing relationship, where words transcend and a true communion unfolds. Through this dialogue, the practitioner realizes that they are not alone on their journey; they are accompanied, supported, and uplifted by angels who hear every whisper of the heart.

In this way, prayer transforms from a simple act into a living bridge, a source of strength, peace, and connection that endures across time, carrying the practitioner into a deeper, richer bond with the angelic realms.

As the practitioner deepens their journey with prayer, they discover it as a dynamic and evolving form of connection, one that reaches beyond structured words into a profound, silent resonance with the angelic realm. Advanced techniques to sustain and enrich this sacred dialogue transform prayer into a daily anchor for spiritual strength, clarity, and comfort. Through these practices, the practitioner cultivates an enduring sense of communion with angels, weaving prayer seamlessly into moments of need, gratitude, and guidance.

In refining the practice of prayer, the practitioner learns the art of quiet listening, a receptive state that follows each prayer's spoken or unspoken words. After expressing their intention, they sit in stillness, opening themselves to the subtle responses of angels. It is in this silence that the practitioner may perceive a gentle warmth, an intuitive insight, or a calm certainty—a language beyond words that conveys angelic presence. These impressions, received in quiet moments, are sacred replies that angels send, as if to say, "We are here with you." By trusting and recording these subtle responses, the practitioner builds a personal archive of angelic messages that offer comfort and guidance over time.

Another advanced practice involves rhythmic breathing as a prelude to prayer, aligning the body and mind to a receptive state. With each breath, the practitioner mentally repeats a simple phrase, such as *"I am open"* on the inhale and *"I receive"* on the exhale. This rhythmic focus harmonizes the energy within, quieting distractions and allowing a clear channel for the prayer's intention. As the practitioner becomes familiar with this rhythmic breathing, they find that it naturally prepares them to sense angelic energies with heightened awareness, creating a steady, calm foundation from which each prayer flows.

Visualization further intensifies the prayer practice, transforming each word or intention into an image or sensation that bridges the spiritual and physical. For example, as they pray for protection, the practitioner envisions a radiant light surrounding them, each word building the light's intensity and reach. In prayers of gratitude, they might visualize waves of golden warmth radiating outward, as if enveloping everything with thanks. This visualization turns prayer into a multi-sensory experience, where each intention is imbued with form and color, making the practitioner's call resonate more powerfully with angels who feel drawn to these vibrant images.

A unique aspect of this deepened practice involves silent or "wordless" prayer, a form of communion that relies solely on the energy of intention without spoken or even mentally formed words. In this practice, the practitioner closes their eyes and visualizes the feeling they wish to convey—such as love, peace, or gratitude—radiating from their heart. They sit quietly, letting this energy grow and extend into the spiritual realm, trusting that angels understand and receive it perfectly. This form of prayer transcends language, becoming a direct transmission of the practitioner's inner state. Angels, attuned to the purity of these energies, respond intuitively, sending their presence as a warm, comforting embrace.

For moments when clarity or direction is needed, the practitioner learns to create questions as part of their prayer, shaping each inquiry with focus and openness. Rather than asking, *"Will you guide me?"* they frame questions as invitations, such as, *"What do I need to see or understand?"* or *"Show me the way forward."* This practice shifts the focus from seeking immediate answers to cultivating an openness to insight. After each question, the practitioner returns to the listening state, attentive to any impressions, images, or feelings that arise. Over time, they recognize that these intuitive responses are gentle nudges from angels, encouraging or reassuring them in ways that resonate deeply with their own heart and spirit.

Incorporating prayer into daily routines is another profound way to sustain angelic connection. Simple, mindful pauses throughout the day—whether before meals, during a walk, or at bedtime—become opportunities for brief moments of gratitude or reflection. Each of these pauses need not be elaborate; a single thought, such as *"Thank you, angels, for your presence today,"* can keep the practitioner in continuous contact. Through these small acts of acknowledgment, they build a rhythm of prayer that transforms ordinary moments into sacred pauses, nourishing the bond with angels throughout all aspects of life.

A written prayer journal is a powerful companion to the practice, serving as a place to document prayers, reflections, and any responses felt or received. The act of writing down a prayer solidifies the intention, allowing the practitioner to revisit it with a sense of continuity and purpose. As they review past entries, they often find patterns in angelic guidance or recurring themes, revealing how the angels have quietly supported their journey. This journal becomes both a sacred record and a source of encouragement, helping the practitioner to see how each prayer has woven a thread of connection, uniting their present with past moments of divine guidance.

Over time, the practitioner may develop personal mantras—short, resonant phrases repeated throughout the day that anchor them in angelic presence. Phrases such as, *"Angels of peace, walk with me,"* or *"I am surrounded by light,"* become touchstones of calm and assurance. These mantras, quietly repeated in moments of stress or transition, act as constant calls to angelic energy, offering strength and serenity when it is most needed. Through the repetition of these sacred phrases, the practitioner finds that the angels' presence feels closer and more immediate, a gentle reminder that they are never truly alone.

In moments of challenge, prayer becomes a powerful means of release, allowing the practitioner to surrender fears, worries, or doubts into angelic hands. By simply stating, *"I release this into your care,"* the practitioner places their burdens with the angels, trusting in their guidance and protection. This act of surrender does not imply passivity but rather a profound faith in angelic wisdom, knowing that sometimes the highest form of prayer is letting go. Through this surrender, the practitioner feels a lightness, as if a weight has been lifted, and a renewed sense of trust that angels will guide the situation in ways beyond immediate understanding.

Group prayers—shared with family, friends, or a spiritual community—amplify the practitioner's individual energy, creating a collective resonance that strengthens each participant's connection to angels. Each voice adds a unique frequency, forming a symphony of intention that reaches out to the angelic realm with magnified strength. In such gatherings, a shared silence often follows the spoken prayers, where everyone present feels the deepening calm and unity, as if a blanket of peace has descended. This shared connection fosters a sense of solidarity, where each participant leaves feeling uplifted, touched by the unified support of both the angels and each other.

As the practitioner integrates these practices, they come to see prayer not just as an occasional request or expression but as a living, breathing connection that continually evolves. Prayer becomes a thread woven through each day's experiences, a way of aligning their spirit with the presence of angels. It transforms from words into a state of being, a feeling of constant companionship, where angels are as present as a heartbeat, always near, always listening, and always ready to guide.

Through these advanced practices, the practitioner discovers that prayer is not an isolated act but a perpetual exchange, a rhythm of giving and receiving that flows seamlessly between themselves and the angels. With each prayer, they step deeper into a world where connection, trust, and divine support form the foundation of their journey, illuminating their path and bringing them ever closer to the light of angelic love.

Chapter 15
Identifying Presence

As the practitioner becomes more attuned to the angelic realm, they begin to recognize subtle signs that reveal an angel's presence—a gentle, almost imperceptible energy that speaks in ways beyond words. These signs manifest in quiet, intuitive ways, like an unseen whisper, and knowing how to perceive them invites a deeper trust in angelic companionship. Guidance on identifying and interpreting these signals helps the practitioner learn to cultivate a quiet awareness of the moments when angels draw near.

The first signs of an angel's presence often come as changes in the physical or sensory environment, delicate shifts that can feel like a warm glow or a cool breeze in the air. The practitioner might notice, for example, a soft warmth encircling them or a sudden sensation of lightness, as if the energy around them has gently lifted. These changes may feel faint, yet they carry a sense of calm and comfort, as though a blanket of serenity has settled upon them. Learning to pause in these moments allows the practitioner to fully experience these subtle cues, tuning their awareness to recognize the peaceful calm that signals an angel's approach.

Another common sign is the presence of light, which may appear as flashes, orbs, or soft glows in the periphery of vision. These lights are usually delicate, a brief shimmer or sparkle that feels out of place in the ordinary setting. Sometimes they seem to dance or flicker, bringing with them a feeling of joy or hope. When the practitioner encounters these lights, they learn to pause, allowing themselves to acknowledge and appreciate these luminous signals as an angelic greeting, a simple yet profound confirmation that angels are near.

Sounds also play a role in revealing angelic presence, often taking the form of subtle tones, gentle chimes, or faint melodies that seem to arise from nowhere. These sounds, delicate yet distinct, resonate in a way that feels harmonious and uplifting. The practitioner may hear a soft ringing or the faintest trace of harp-like notes, sounds that seem woven from light itself. These auditory signs are invitations to pause, listen, and tune into the deeper layers of reality where angelic beings reside. By appreciating these gentle tones as sacred signals, the practitioner nurtures an openness to receive even clearer forms of angelic communication.

Beyond the physical, angels also communicate through sensations, impressions that arise within the body as if responding to the presence of a beloved friend. A sudden warmth in the chest, a tingling on the skin, or an unexplainable feeling of peace that seems to radiate from within—each sensation speaks of angelic energy. The practitioner may also feel a sense of being lightly touched on the shoulder or a gentle pressure on the back, as if an angel is there, offering silent support. With time and attentiveness, these sensations become a familiar language, a wordless connection that assures the practitioner of their angel's comforting presence.

Angels also communicate by inspiring specific thoughts or images that seem to arise spontaneously. In moments of reflection or prayer, the practitioner may notice unexpected images in their mind—a serene landscape, a comforting face, or a symbol of peace. These are not random thoughts; rather, they are visual messages intended to soothe, reassure, or guide. By paying attention to these impressions, the practitioner learns to recognize how angels use mental imagery as a gentle form of guidance, each image carrying a meaning that resonates with the heart.

Feathers, especially white ones, are among the most recognizable signs of angelic presence. When found unexpectedly, they serve as gentle reminders, placed in the practitioner's path as if by unseen hands. Each feather, delicate and pure, symbolizes protection, love, and angelic watchfulness. When the practitioner discovers a feather in an unlikely place—a doorstep, a window ledge, or even indoors—they acknowledge it as a quiet message, a reminder that angels are watching over them. Collecting these feathers or keeping them in a special place on the altar reinforces the sense of angelic closeness.

Synchronicities, meaningful coincidences, are another way angels subtly communicate. These can take many forms: a particular number sequence seen repeatedly, a song with a comforting message that plays at a perfect moment, or a phrase overheard that answers an inner question. These synchronicities carry a feeling of magic, a reminder that the universe, with angels' guidance, is orchestrating events in ways that support the practitioner's path. Recognizing these moments as angelic signs encourages the practitioner to trust that they are being guided, each synchronicity a gentle nudge toward alignment with divine timing and purpose.

Floral scents, especially in spaces without any visible source, are often associated with angelic presence. The practitioner may suddenly sense the fragrance of roses, jasmine, or lilies, smells that feel out of place in the physical environment yet linger with a sense of serenity and beauty. These scents arrive as subtle blessings, gentle reminders that angels surround the practitioner with love and grace. Each time they catch a hint of these unexpected aromas, they pause to breathe in, honoring it as a sacred greeting from the angels.

Another profound experience of presence is an inner calm that arises spontaneously, especially during moments of distress or anxiety. The practitioner may find that a wave of peace descends upon them, calming their thoughts and filling their heart with reassurance. This tranquility, gentle yet profound, is the angel's way of offering support and strength, bringing the practitioner back to a state of balance. Embracing this calm helps the practitioner to realize that angels respond not only to calls for help but to every moment of need, offering comfort that is both immediate and profound.

Dreams often serve as channels for angelic messages, where symbols, colors, or direct guidance appear in ways that speak to the subconscious. In dreams, the practitioner may see figures of light, hear words of encouragement, or receive insights that resonate with their waking life. By keeping a dream journal, they can document these experiences, noting recurring themes or symbols that emerge over time. Reviewing these dreams reveals a deeper dialogue, a pattern of angelic communication that speaks to the practitioner's ongoing spiritual journey.

The practitioner learns that angels often reveal their presence through an unexplainable feeling of love, a warmth that fills the heart and soul with a sense of connection and belonging. This feeling is beyond ordinary emotion, carrying a depth and purity that feels like a divine embrace. In these moments, the practitioner experiences what can only be described as pure love, a reminder of the angelic guidance that accompanies them every step of the way. This love becomes a cornerstone, a reminder that the angels' presence is real, constant, and woven into the very fabric of their journey.

In learning to recognize these signs, the practitioner develops an intuitive awareness that goes beyond the senses, a deep knowing that angels are near. This awareness brings a new dimension to life, where the veil between worlds feels thinner, and each day holds moments of divine connection. With each sign, angels reassure the practitioner that they are seen, heard, and protected, affirming the quiet but profound truth that they are never alone.

Through this journey of perception, the practitioner realizes that angelic presence is not reserved for extraordinary moments but is woven into the fabric of daily life, awaiting recognition in every quiet glance, every peaceful breath, every unexpected sign. By embracing these subtle cues, they deepen their understanding of angelic guidance, drawing ever closer to the beings who walk beside them, ever-present and ready to support with love and light.

As the practitioner deepens their sensitivity to angelic presence, they discover that these subtle signs go beyond mere indications; they become part of a nuanced dialogue, a form of guidance and support that gently unfolds with each interaction. Further exploration into recognizing and interpreting angelic signals offers insights and practices to help the practitioner build a confident understanding of these signs. By honing their perception, they learn to differentiate angelic energies from other influences, cultivating a connection that feels intimate, personal, and profoundly reassuring.

One of the first steps in deepening this perception is learning to trust intuition. Angelic signs often align closely with intuitive feelings, arriving as spontaneous insights or gut sensations that arise without logical explanation. The practitioner may sense a "knowing" that appears fully formed—a feeling of confidence about a decision, a quiet urge to pursue a particular path, or a gentle caution to pause. By embracing these moments of clarity and recognizing them as possible angelic guidance, the practitioner learns to trust their inner sense. Over time, intuition becomes a companion, a reliable guide that brings the comfort of angelic wisdom into everyday choices.

To distinguish angelic signs from other energies, the practitioner can use simple grounding techniques, such as deep breathing or visualization, to clear their mind before interpreting any impressions. By taking a few deep breaths, the practitioner centers their energy, allowing them to sense the difference between true angelic messages—filled with peace, love, and clarity—and energies that feel heavier, unclear, or distracting. This practice of grounding before interpreting impressions helps create a "clean slate" of awareness, one that is open yet discerning, guiding the practitioner to sense the purity of angelic presence more reliably.

An additional layer of perception involves becoming aware of temperature shifts, often more pronounced during moments of angelic connection. Angels, being high-vibrational beings, can subtly alter the surrounding energy. The practitioner may notice a warm, gentle feeling that seems to surround them or, conversely, a cooling sensation, like a soft breeze touching the skin. These temperature changes often accompany feelings of comfort and calm, reassuring them that they are in the presence of angels. Each time they feel this shift, the practitioner pauses, allowing their awareness to focus on the feeling, learning to recognize it as a loving confirmation of angelic proximity.

In practicing patience and receptivity, the practitioner begins to recognize that angelic signs can sometimes unfold gradually, like a story told over days or even weeks. For instance, a specific symbol—a feather, a number, or a recurring image—might appear repeatedly, forming a thread that only reveals its meaning over time. This slow unfolding encourages the practitioner to remain open and attentive, like piecing together parts of a puzzle. Each sign, when viewed with patience, becomes part of a larger message, as if the angels are guiding the practitioner with gentle reminders, urging them to observe the message's development.

Further, the practitioner learns to interpret recurring numbers, often seen as a form of angelic communication that provides clarity and reassurance. Common sequences, such as 111, 444, or 777, carry unique meanings often connected with spiritual growth, protection, or divine support. For example, 111 might signify alignment with purpose, while 444 could indicate that angels are present to offer support. As these numbers appear repeatedly, the practitioner interprets them as encouragement, reminders that their journey is supported. By becoming familiar with these number sequences, they develop an awareness of how angels communicate directly through symbols that resonate with both their intuition and experience.

Another advanced practice is engaging with the sensations of touch as a form of angelic presence. The practitioner may experience a feeling as delicate as a hand resting on the shoulder, a brush against the cheek, or a soft touch on the hand. These sensations, though subtle, are deeply personal, as if the angels are offering physical reassurance. Each touch carries a feeling of warmth and calm, often arriving when the practitioner needs comfort or encouragement most. By recognizing these experiences as gentle acts of support, they strengthen their confidence in angelic companionship.

In moments of heightened awareness, angels may communicate through direct thoughts or phrases that enter the mind unexpectedly. These thoughts carry a clarity and simplicity that feels distinct, often brief yet profound. For example, during a difficult decision, the practitioner may suddenly hear a phrase like *"Trust your heart"* or *"You are not alone."* These messages arrive quietly, almost as if whispered within, resonating with a wisdom that feels beyond ordinary thought. By noting these clear thoughts and honoring them as angelic guidance, the practitioner develops a confidence that angels communicate through their innermost thoughts, offering insights that are timely, supportive, and reassuring.

Sensing angelic presence in nature is another powerful experience for the practitioner, who may feel a heightened sense of connection when surrounded by natural beauty. In places where light, color, and life are abundant—a sunlit forest, a peaceful lake, a garden in bloom—the practitioner finds that angelic presence becomes more tangible, like a natural infusion of peace and joy. During these moments, they feel a unique sense of unity, as if the angels are using the beauty of nature to amplify their message of love and support. By seeking these moments in nature, the practitioner nurtures an environment where angelic communication feels clear, creating a space where the divine and earthly meet.

To refine their perception, the practitioner may also practice intentional quietude, taking a few minutes each day to sit in silence with the intention of sensing angelic presence. In this quiet space, they listen not only with the mind but with the heart, allowing feelings, impressions, and even small shifts in energy to arise naturally. This quiet practice becomes a sacred time, a daily opportunity to strengthen their attunement to angelic energies. Through consistent quietude, the practitioner becomes more adept at distinguishing the gentle nuances of angelic presence, learning to sense the distinct qualities that angels bring.

Meditation enhances these practices by creating a calm, receptive state where angelic signs can be experienced with clarity. During meditation, the practitioner focuses on breathing, visualizing a soft light within that expands to welcome angelic energy. In this calm state, they may sense tingling, warmth, or a gentle light filling the mind's eye, all indicators of an angel's presence. Each meditation becomes a space where they invite angels to draw near, a sacred practice that builds a foundation for sensing their guidance. Over time, the practitioner finds that meditative practice makes it easier to recognize angelic signals in everyday life, each experience confirming the profound, loving connection they share.

In deepening these practices, the practitioner realizes that identifying angelic presence is as much about inner openness as it is about outer signs. Through intuition, patience, and a willingness to trust, they create a steady dialogue with angels, a communion that brings guidance, comfort, and a sense of divine companionship. Each sign, no matter how subtle, becomes a source of reassurance, a reminder that angels walk beside them, supporting each step of their journey with boundless love and gentle wisdom.

By embracing these practices, the practitioner steps fully into the mystery of angelic connection, recognizing that each sign is a gift, a reflection of divine care that brings peace and joy. This awareness transforms their journey, for in sensing angels nearby, they come to feel that life itself is woven with unseen grace, where every sign is an invitation to trust, believe, and walk forward in the light of angelic presence.

Chapter 16
Gratitude Ritual

In the tapestry of angelic connection, gratitude becomes a radiant thread that binds the practitioner's intentions with the divine presence surrounding them. The practice of a gratitude ritual unfolds, where heartfelt thanks serve as an invitation for angels to draw closer, weaving bonds that are strengthened by acknowledgment and appreciation. With each gesture of gratitude, the practitioner opens a channel for deeper interaction, creating an environment where angelic guidance flows freely and abundantly.

The ritual of gratitude begins with a simple yet powerful acknowledgment of the unseen forces at work, offering thanks for the guidance and protection received throughout life's journey. This appreciation sets the tone, awakening a profound awareness of the blessings that often go unnoticed. In preparing for the ritual, the practitioner may choose to arrange a few symbolic items in a sacred space, each item representing a facet of their gratitude—perhaps a candle symbolizing light in dark times, a feather representing angelic guidance, or a crystal that has aided in spiritual clarity. These objects create a focal point, grounding their intentions in the physical realm as they begin their practice.

To deepen the sense of reverence, the practitioner may begin with a grounding meditation, bringing their attention inward to calm the mind and center the heart. With each breath, they visualize gratitude flowing from within, filling their heart with a warm, gentle light. As this light expands, it radiates outward, enveloping the room and reaching toward the unseen realm where angels dwell. This light becomes a bridge, carrying the practitioner's gratitude beyond the material world and into the spiritual, creating a connection that resonates with love and appreciation.

An essential part of the gratitude ritual is expressing thanks for both tangible and intangible blessings—the quiet guidance that steers life's course, the signs and synchronicities that bring reassurance, and even the challenges that foster growth. As the practitioner reflects on these aspects, they may speak their gratitude aloud, letting their words resonate with sincerity. A spoken affirmation like, *"I thank you for the guidance you have provided and for walking beside me on this journey,"* strengthens the intention, sending a clear, heartfelt message to the angels who listen with an ever-present attentiveness.

Writing can also be woven into the ritual, creating a gratitude list that captures moments when angelic support was felt most deeply. Each entry is a memory, a gentle reminder of times when the practitioner felt lifted, inspired, or protected. By writing these experiences down, the practitioner reinforces their connection to the angels who have been present throughout these moments. This list becomes a sacred document, one that can be revisited during times of doubt or uncertainty, serving as a testament to the unwavering support received from the angelic realm.

Candles hold a special place in the gratitude ritual, acting as beacons of light that guide one's intentions to the spiritual realm. The practitioner may light a candle, dedicating its glow as an offering of appreciation to the angels. As the flame dances, they focus on the warmth it emits, imagining it as a symbol of their gratitude, flickering across the boundaries between the physical and ethereal. Watching the flame, they allow feelings of appreciation to expand, flowing freely and reaching out to the angels who gather near, drawn by the sincerity of the practitioner's intentions.

To amplify their gratitude, the practitioner may choose to incorporate angelic symbols, such as placing a small feather or crystal upon the altar as a representation of angelic presence. Holding these items, they let feelings of appreciation flow, honoring these sacred tokens as reminders of the protection, love, and guidance that angels provide. Each symbol, imbued with the energy of gratitude, serves as a tangible link to the angelic realm, creating a bridge that keeps the practitioner connected to divine assistance.

Music or sound can further enhance the ritual, inviting harmonious vibrations that resonate with the angelic frequencies. The practitioner may play soft, soothing music or gently ring a bell, allowing the tones to echo through their sacred space. These sounds serve as a call, a way of acknowledging the presence of angels and expressing appreciation for their constant, unwavering support. As the sounds fade, the practitioner sits in silence, allowing the reverberations to carry their gratitude into the stillness, filling the room with a sense of peace and calm.

In closing the ritual, the practitioner takes a moment to silently reflect, holding a space of quiet reverence and appreciation. With a deep breath, they release their gratitude, sending it outward as an offering to the angels who have walked with them on this path. This final gesture is one of trust and surrender, knowing that their gratitude has been felt, acknowledged, and welcomed by the angels who continue to watch over them.

As a regular practice, the gratitude ritual becomes a way to cultivate a continual connection with the angelic realm. By incorporating it into their routine, the practitioner invites angels to remain ever-present in their life, responding to the warmth of appreciation with renewed guidance and protection. Each repetition of the ritual strengthens this bond, creating an atmosphere where angelic energies are invited to flourish, filling the practitioner's life with grace, support, and a constant sense of being divinely held.

In the journey of spiritual growth, gratitude becomes a pathway, a means of drawing nearer to the wisdom and love that angels offer so freely. Through this ritual, the practitioner not only honors the angels but also nourishes their own spirit, awakening to the blessings that surround them in every moment. With each expression of thanks, they deepen their awareness of a truth as old as time—that they are never alone, that angels walk with them, and that their life is touched by an infinite, unseen grace.

The journey of gratitude extends beyond a single ritual, deepening into a practice that permeates every moment of the practitioner's life. As gratitude becomes a continuous bond with the angelic realm, each expression of thanks becomes a new point of connection. Through regular practices of thanksgiving, the practitioner reinforces their relationship with angels, creating an open channel for ongoing support, guidance, and protection.

One powerful approach to maintaining this connection is through the establishment of daily or weekly moments of gratitude, simple yet intentional reflections that acknowledge the presence and support of angels. These moments do not require a formal ritual space; instead, they can be woven into everyday routines, such as the quiet time before sleep, moments in nature, or even a brief pause during a busy day. Each instance becomes a reminder of the companionship of angels, keeping their influence alive and active in the practitioner's awareness.

To build a deeper rhythm of gratitude, the practitioner may consider starting each day with a small, intentional act of appreciation. In the morning light, before the demands of the day begin, they can pause, placing a hand over their heart and silently thanking the angels for the strength, clarity, and guidance to come. This brief act sets a tone of openness and receptivity, aligning the practitioner's energy with angelic presence and inviting their support into the day's experiences. By making this a daily habit, gratitude becomes a natural part of their morning, awakening a mindful connection that remains throughout the day.

As an extension of the gratitude ritual, the practitioner might also keep a gratitude journal, a sacred place to document encounters with angelic presence and record moments of divine guidance and protection. Each entry becomes a tangible reflection of their spiritual journey, preserving memories of guidance received, challenges overcome, and synchronicities that affirm the angels' watchful care. With each entry, the journal grows into a treasured record, one that holds the practitioner's relationship with their angels in pages of gratitude and reflection.

Beyond individual expressions, group gratitude rituals can magnify the energy of thanks, bringing together loved ones to share and celebrate angelic guidance. In a circle of trust and unity, participants may take turns expressing gratitude for the angelic support felt in their lives, creating a shared intention that resonates deeply. As each person voices their appreciation, the collective energy forms a powerful channel of light, amplifying their connection to the angelic realm. This gathering of souls, joined in gratitude, invites angels to draw near, filling the space with a warmth and radiance that each participant can carry forward in their own journey.

To enrich these practices, the practitioner may explore sacred symbols and gestures to express their gratitude more fully. By incorporating symbols like angelic sigils, feathers, or chosen crystals, they create visual representations of their thanks, reinforcing their intentions through objects that hold spiritual meaning. Over time, these symbols become infused with the energy of gratitude, acting as tangible reminders of the practitioner's connection to the angels. Whether placed on an altar, carried as a personal token, or used during prayer, these symbols keep the practitioner's gratitude alive in the physical realm, bridging the unseen and the seen.

Meditative visualization adds another layer, enabling the practitioner to create a mental landscape where they can engage directly with angelic presence. In a state of calm reflection, they can imagine themselves surrounded by a soft, radiant light, feeling the warmth of their angels around them. Within this light, they mentally express their thanks, watching as their words of gratitude transform into beams that rise, like golden threads, to connect with the angelic realm. This visualization not only reinforces their intention but also serves as a moment of inner peace, where gratitude becomes a quiet sanctuary shared with their angels.

In times of challenge or uncertainty, gratitude can be a powerful anchor, transforming moments of fear or doubt into spaces of calm trust. When the practitioner finds themselves facing difficulties, they can pause and bring to mind past moments where angelic support has lifted them. This remembrance acts as a wellspring of strength, reassuring them that they are not alone, even in times of trial. By drawing on these memories, they build a resilient faith in their angelic companions, creating a sense of inner stability rooted in trust and gratitude.

Regularly renewing vows of gratitude strengthens this spiritual connection, making it a constant in the practitioner's life. These vows can be as simple as a promise to acknowledge angelic presence, to remain open to their guidance, or to practice gratitude as a form of devotion. With each vow, the practitioner reaffirms their commitment to their spiritual path, transforming gratitude from a single act into an enduring state of being. These vows act as threads that weave through the fabric of their life, creating an unbreakable connection with their angels, who respond to this commitment with ever-deeper guidance and support.

In the practice of gratitude, the practitioner ultimately learns to view every moment as an opportunity to connect with angels. The natural world becomes filled with symbols of angelic presence—sunlight filtering through trees, the gentle flight of a bird, the whisper of wind. By recognizing these signs as divine reminders, the practitioner cultivates an awareness that the angels are not distant beings but are woven into the very essence of life itself. Each sight, sound, and experience becomes a doorway to deeper connection, an invitation to pause and appreciate the beauty of divine companionship.

Moving beyond formal rituals, the practitioner begins to embrace gratitude as a way of life, becoming attuned to the angelic presence that surrounds them, sensing it in each small blessing and act of kindness. Through this expanded awareness, gratitude transforms from an action into a state of grace—a constant communion with the angels that fills the heart with peace, wonder, and joy.

In this journey, the practitioner discovers that gratitude is more than a gesture; it is a path that leads them to a profound truth: that they are surrounded, supported, and deeply loved by their angels, who respond to every sincere expression of thanks with a love that transcends time and space.

Chapter 17
Seeking Guidance in Dreams

As the night descends and the world quiets, a doorway opens to a realm where angelic guidance flows more freely, where whispers from the divine can reach the receptive soul. In dreams, the boundaries of the conscious mind soften, allowing angels to communicate through symbols, visions, and impressions that carry profound insights. Guidance is offered to lead the practitioner into this sacred space, teaching practices that prepare the mind and spirit to receive messages from angels during sleep.

To begin this journey, the practitioner creates a nightly ritual that signals their intention to connect with angels in the dream state. This preparation starts with a calming routine that invites peace into the body and quiets the thoughts. Lighting a small candle or placing a comforting object, like a favorite crystal or feather, by the bedside can help set the stage. Each night, these objects serve as reminders of the presence of angelic energies close by, creating an environment where the practitioner feels safe and open to receiving guidance.

Setting an intention is the next key step, one that gently directs the focus and energy of the practitioner's dreams. In the moments before sleep, they may silently state their intention, speaking words like, *"I invite my angels to bring me guidance in my dreams. I am open to receiving messages of clarity and peace."* This clear expression of intent signals a readiness to accept angelic insights, while also establishing a spiritual boundary of protection and positivity. The practitioner may repeat this intention each night, creating a steady rhythm of openness and trust.

To enhance the connection, visualizations offer a powerful way to invite angelic presence. As the practitioner lies in bed, they may imagine a soft, radiant light surrounding them, a cocoon of warmth and serenity. Within this light, they envision angelic figures nearby, their presence soothing and filled with love. With each breath, the practitioner lets go of the day's concerns, sinking deeper into this comforting light, feeling themselves drift closer to the threshold of dreams where angelic messages await.

Journaling plays a vital role in recording and understanding the messages received. Upon waking, the practitioner can reach for a journal kept by the bedside, capturing any fragments of memory, images, or feelings that linger from their dreams. No detail is too small or insignificant, as dreams often communicate through subtle symbols that only reveal their meaning through reflection and patience. By writing down these impressions immediately, the practitioner honors the messages, preserving them for later analysis and interpretation.

Dream symbols often hold layers of meaning, many of which reveal themselves through repeated patterns over time. For instance, seeing images of light, birds, or open doors might symbolize freedom, guidance, or new opportunities encouraged by angelic presence. Similarly, feelings of warmth, peace, or joy in dreams can indicate moments of true connection with angelic energies. As the practitioner reviews their dream journal, patterns begin to emerge, revealing themes that the angels wish to communicate, each layer adding depth to their understanding of these nocturnal messages.

For those who seek a deeper connection, using crystals under the pillow or near the bed can enhance receptivity to spiritual messages. Stones such as amethyst or celestite are particularly powerful allies, known for their calming and clarifying properties. When placed nearby during sleep, these crystals create a peaceful energy field that aligns with the angelic realm, amplifying the practitioner's openness to guidance. Over time, these stones become conduits of spiritual energy, enhancing the clarity and vividness of the dreams received.

In addition to setting intentions, prayers are a valuable tool for inviting angelic support into the dream space. The practitioner may say a quiet prayer before sleep, asking for protection, clarity, and guidance. A prayer like, *"I ask for my guardian angels to watch over me as I sleep and to bring me wisdom through my dreams. Let me awaken with understanding and peace,"* reinforces the invitation, aligning the practitioner's energy with angelic presence and creating a bridge between their conscious and subconscious mind.

Not all dreams offer direct answers, and the practitioner learns to trust in the unfolding process, understanding that guidance often arrives over several nights or even weeks. As they continue this nightly practice, they begin to notice how certain dreams bring a sense of clarity or reassurance, while others might present symbols that require thoughtful reflection. The practitioner embraces this gradual awakening to angelic guidance, trusting that each dream offers a stepping stone along their spiritual path.

Developing sensitivity to intuitive feelings that arise upon waking helps deepen the interpretation of angelic messages. Sometimes, the practitioner may wake with a lingering feeling of peace, joy, or encouragement that cannot be traced to a specific dream image. This feeling itself is a message, a reminder from the angels that they have offered guidance, even if the details are not immediately recalled. The practitioner learns to trust these impressions, allowing them to guide their day and nurture an ongoing connection with the angelic realm.

As dream messages accumulate in the journal, the practitioner gains insight not only into the angels' messages but also into their own soul's journey. These nighttime encounters become a mirror, reflecting truths that the conscious mind might overlook. With time and practice, the practitioner grows attuned to the wisdom embedded in their dreams, feeling a sense of trust and companionship with their angels that carries forward into their waking life.

Dreams, in this practice, become not just a sequence of images but a living language of light, through which angels communicate gently yet profoundly. As the practitioner continues their nightly ritual of seeking guidance, they step into a world where night and day blend, where angels walk beside them, and where the wisdom of dreams brings peace, comfort, and a quiet assurance that they are held in love.

With each night, the practice of seeking guidance in dreams grows richer, evolving into a realm of profound communion where the lines between earthly experience and angelic insight blur. To deepen this practice, the practitioner engages in methods that refine their capacity to remember, interpret, and harness the wisdom offered through dreams. Advanced techniques for recording, understanding, and interpreting angelic messages that surface within the dream state invite the practitioner to uncover a personal dialogue with the divine.

One of the most powerful practices for deepening dream work is establishing a dream journal that acts not only as a record but as a reflective space for examining patterns, symbols, and insights over time. The practitioner begins by organizing their journal entries in a way that allows for easy review. Dividing pages by date or using colored markers to highlight recurring themes helps create a more structured approach. Patterns become easier to identify, and over weeks or months, symbols that might once have seemed fragmented begin to weave together into a coherent narrative of guidance.

Recording dreams involves more than jotting down images or snippets of memory. The practitioner learns to capture the tone, emotional nuances, and any physical sensations upon waking, which can offer subtle clues to angelic presence. For instance, a dream in which the practitioner feels surrounded by a warm, comforting light might indicate an encounter with guardian angels. Meanwhile, symbols like open pathways, wings, or celestial landscapes often suggest angelic encouragement and support. By noting these subtle aspects, the practitioner builds a comprehensive picture of the dream's energy, leading to a clearer understanding of the angelic messages at play.

Developing sensitivity to the emotional resonance of each dream is essential. Sometimes, the message is embedded not in specific imagery but in the feeling that lingers upon waking—a sense of clarity, a feeling of peace, or even a strong desire to take a particular action. These intuitive responses are valuable threads in the web of angelic communication. The practitioner is encouraged to follow these feelings, noting any inner promptings or realizations that arise in the hours following the dream, as these impressions often continue to unfold in daily life, enriching the dream's message with added layers of guidance.

To further enhance dream recall, the practitioner may incorporate rituals of alignment before sleep. These could involve gentle breathing exercises, energy-clearing practices, or meditative visualization to create a receptive mental state. One effective method is visualizing a serene, celestial landscape—a meadow bathed in starlight, a quiet temple surrounded by radiant light, or a pathway of golden steps leading upwards. As they imagine this space, they mentally invite their angels to join them, symbolically opening the doorway for angelic presence to communicate more freely through the night.

Preparing the physical space of the dream journal ritual adds another dimension to the practice. Some practitioners choose to consecrate their journals, perhaps placing it on a small altar or surrounding it with symbols of light and angelic presence—crystals, a white candle, or angelic sigils. Each night, they may open the journal with a brief prayer or intention, asking for clarity and understanding. This act deepens their commitment, making the journal a living artifact of their spiritual journey and a focal point where earthly intention and divine insight meet.

Another advanced technique involves creating a dream recall mantra. Before sleep, the practitioner can repeat a simple phrase such as, "I remember and understand my dreams," letting the words settle into their subconscious as a gentle command. This mantra helps prime the mind for recall and, when practiced consistently, strengthens the practitioner's ability to retain even the subtlest aspects of their dreams. Over time, this practice heightens dream clarity, enabling them to wake with vivid details and a stronger grasp of the messages received.

In interpreting dreams, recognizing individual symbols that hold personal meaning is invaluable. The practitioner reflects upon what certain objects or colors signify to them personally—whether water feels purifying, or light represents protection, or a bridge suggests transition. By associating personal meanings with these symbols, the practitioner deciphers dreams in a way that resonates deeply with their own experiences and intuitions. Often, angelic messages manifest through symbols that align with the practitioner's unique perspective, making personal insight an essential tool for understanding dreams.

Regular review sessions offer a way to deepen this understanding, allowing the practitioner to revisit past entries with fresh eyes. Every few weeks, they can spend time reading through prior entries, taking note of recurring symbols, colors, or themes that appear over time. By doing so, they create a bridge between each night's insight and the broader spiritual journey, noticing how certain messages repeat, intensify, or evolve. This ongoing analysis nurtures a personal connection with angelic guidance, revealing an intricate web of wisdom and support that weaves through the practitioner's life.

In moments when clarity is elusive, the practitioner may seek guidance through meditative reflection, a practice that allows them to return to the dream in a state of calm receptivity. During quiet meditation, they can recall the dream as vividly as possible, allowing additional details or emotions to surface. Sometimes, the conscious mind needs a moment of stillness to reconnect with the intuitive insights first felt in the dream state. Through this process, the practitioner taps into deeper layers of meaning, bringing to light messages that might have remained hidden at first glance.

Advanced dreamwork also encourages the practitioner to invite specific types of guidance. For example, if facing a particular life question, they may state a clear request before sleep: *"My angels, I ask for insight into the path ahead. Show me through my dreams what I need to understand."* By aligning their intention with a specific question, they create a focused invitation for angelic guidance. Though answers may not appear in a single night, the practitioner remains patient, knowing that the angels will respond in time and that the dream space will become a realm of illumination.

As the practice reaches a point of deeper understanding, the practitioner realizes that angelic guidance through dreams is a gentle unfolding, a process that mirrors the journey of awakening itself. In dreams, messages come through symbols, emotions, and impressions that require patience and reverence to fully decipher. The practice of seeking guidance in dreams becomes a mirror of the practitioner's openness to divine influence in every facet of their life, night and day intertwined, each feeding the other in a cycle of learning and growth.

In these nightly journeys, they find reassurance that their angels are ever-present, guiding them along the path of their soul's highest purpose. As they deepen this practice, they step closer to a truth that shines brightly through each dream: that they are deeply loved, watched over, and guided by angels, whose wisdom fills even the silent spaces of sleep with light, peace, and timeless understanding.

Chapter 18
Angels and the Lunar Cycle

In the silent rhythm of the moon's phases, there exists a sacred alignment that resonates with the celestial forces around us. Each shift in the lunar cycle—its waxing, full, waning, and new phases—carries an energy that subtly influences all of life. For those attuned to the angelic realm, the lunar cycle serves as a bridge, amplifying their connection with angels and enhancing rituals of healing, guidance, and intention. Exploring the mysteries of aligning angelic practices with the lunar cycle invites the practitioner to step into a harmonious flow with the universe's natural rhythms.

In the days of the waxing moon, when the lunar light gradually grows, an expansive energy fills the air, favoring the setting of intentions and the calling forth of new guidance. Angels who oversee growth and clarity, such as Archangel Uriel, whose light illuminates knowledge, can be invoked during this phase. The practitioner begins by reflecting on what they wish to cultivate in their spiritual path, perhaps seeking insight into a new direction, a clearer understanding, or the strength to begin a journey. Invocations during this period focus on guidance and enlightenment, with the practitioner affirming intentions aligned with spiritual growth.

To engage with the waxing moon's energies, the practitioner might prepare a ritual that emphasizes light, envisioning their intentions as a growing flame that reflects the moon's increasing illumination. Lighting a candle and focusing on its gentle radiance, they allow their intentions to rise within them, feeling the energy amplify as they call upon angelic presence to guide them in their pursuits. By repeating their intentions quietly, they synchronize their energies with the expansive quality of the waxing moon, establishing a receptive connection with angels who aid in their quest for knowledge, healing, or transformation.

When the moon reaches its fullness, a time of culmination and heightened energy unfolds, enhancing angelic rituals with a powerful sense of manifestation. The full moon illuminates all things hidden, making it an ideal time for requesting clarity from angels or seeking answers to complex questions. Archangel Gabriel, the messenger, is often associated with the full moon, as his energy facilitates communication and divine insight. This is an opportunity for the practitioner to bring their desires, fears, or questions fully into the light, trusting that the angels will offer clarity and guidance.

During a full moon ritual, the practitioner may choose to sit outside under the moonlight, absorbing its energy and focusing on openness and receptivity. Holding a crystal known to enhance intuition—such as amethyst or moonstone—they silently invite their angels to communicate whatever wisdom or insight they need at this time. The moon's brightness serves as a beacon, helping them see their intentions clearly and allowing angelic messages to reach them with greater depth. As they reflect, the practitioner may feel the presence of angelic energies surrounding them, offering a sense of completion, harmony, and divine guidance.

The waning moon brings a shift, as the moonlight begins to recede and the focus turns to release and letting go. This phase invites the practitioner to reflect on aspects of their life, habits, or thoughts that may hinder their spiritual growth. Archangel Michael, known for his strength and protection, is a powerful ally during this time. His energy aids in releasing negativity, clearing away blockages, and creating space for new intentions to blossom. The practitioner focuses on surrendering what no longer serves them, allowing the moon's gentle waning energy to carry these burdens away.

To embrace the waning moon's influence, the practitioner can create a ritual of release. Sitting quietly, they visualize the energies or emotions they wish to let go, watching them dissolve into the soft darkness of the night. Holding a symbol of protection—a feather, a protective crystal, or a candle representing Archangel Michael's light—they ask for angelic assistance in their release. With each breath, they feel the weight lessen, and with each exhale, they entrust their burdens to the angels. This gentle letting go aligns with the moon's withdrawal, creating space within for the divine presence to move freely.

The cycle concludes with the new moon, a time of rest, renewal, and quiet introspection. In this darkened phase, when the moon is hidden from sight, the practitioner turns inward, connecting with angels in a space of stillness and surrender. This phase is ideal for setting quiet, heartfelt intentions, grounding oneself, and listening to the subtler messages of the angelic realm. Angels of peace and inner guidance, such as Archangel Raphael, lend their soothing energy, assisting the practitioner in replenishing and grounding their spirit.

In a new moon ritual, the practitioner creates a sacred space by clearing any lingering energies, perhaps with sage or gentle music. Sitting in stillness, they focus on breathing deeply, entering a state of relaxation and openness. With each breath, they affirm a fresh beginning, allowing themselves to feel the quiet promise of renewal that the angels and the moon offer. Holding their hands over their heart, they invite Archangel Raphael to fill their being with a gentle light that heals and restores. In this sacred silence, the practitioner embraces the new moon's gift of introspection and reconnection, finding a deep peace within.

Aligning angelic practices with the lunar cycle is not only a means of connecting with angels but also a way of stepping into harmony with the universe's natural rhythm. Each phase offers a unique invitation to deepen the bond with angelic energies, to listen, to release, and to renew. The practitioner who honors these phases finds their connection with the angels enriched, guided by the cosmic flow that extends beyond the earth into the heavens.

In these quiet, celestial rhythms, the practitioner experiences the profound support of angelic presence, each cycle a gentle reminder of the never-ending renewal available on the spiritual path. Through the luminous language of the moon, angels speak, guiding, protecting, and loving, as they walk alongside the soul in every phase of life.

The journey with angels through the lunar cycle deepens as each phase reveals specific practices for fostering harmony and enhancing spiritual awareness. Further exploration into aligning angelic connections with the moon's phases offers intentional rituals tailored to each phase's unique energy, inviting angelic wisdom into every stage of renewal, growth, and transformation.

As the moon begins its waxing phase, there is a profound momentum building within the practitioner—a time to plant seeds of intention and envision growth. This is an ideal period to initiate intentions with the support of angels known for wisdom, courage, and manifestation. Angels like Archangel Jophiel, often associated with beauty, creativity, and clarity, assist in illuminating the pathway ahead. Practitioners may write their intentions or goals on small slips of paper, focusing on what they seek to grow in their lives. Each intention is infused with a blessing, visualizing it filled with the soft, expanding glow of the waxing moon, symbolizing its journey into fullness.

To enhance this practice, the practitioner can place the intention slips under a crystal, such as citrine, known for amplifying goals and manifestation, while softly invoking angelic support. By keeping these intentions visible—either on an altar or a dedicated space—the practitioner is reminded of their unfolding journey and is open to angelic messages that may come during this time, often through dreams or intuitive insights. Each day, they nurture these intentions with affirmations, aligning with the growing moon and angelic presence to draw their vision closer to reality.

At the full moon, angelic connection reaches a peak, offering potent energies for manifestation, clarity, and deepened spiritual insight. This is a powerful time to engage in a moonlit ceremony with Archangel Gabriel, the messenger angel, whose presence assists in receiving clarity and communicating intentions to the divine. Standing outside under the full moon, the practitioner absorbs the lunar energy, feeling it infuse every aspect of their being. They may offer prayers or speak their intentions aloud, allowing the light of the moon to illuminate their words and guide them toward angelic understanding.

In this state of openness, they can engage in a reflective practice known as the "Moon's Mirror." Holding a mirror under the moonlight, the practitioner gazes at their reflection, asking the angels to reveal what they need to see in their life or within themselves. This symbolic act encourages self-awareness, illuminating truths and deeper meanings that may have remained hidden. Often, angelic messages at the full moon reveal profound insights that help the practitioner understand their path more clearly, as if the angels are whispering truths through the silvery light.

As the moon wanes, the energy subtly shifts toward release and introspection, a time for letting go of energies that may impede the path forward. In this phase, the practitioner can turn to Archangel Michael, whose presence offers protection, strength, and the courage to release that which no longer serves. A cleansing ritual during this period might include writing down habits, fears, or attachments that the practitioner is ready to release. These words can then be symbolically burned in a small fire or dissolved in a bowl of water, visualizing them releasing fully.

During this ritual, the practitioner might place a hand over their heart, asking Archangel Michael to cut energetic cords that bind them to anything that no longer serves their highest purpose. As the practitioner breathes deeply, they envision the gentle removal of these attachments, feeling lighter and more aligned with their true self. Through this symbolic release, the practitioner makes space within, a sacred clearing for the presence of angels and for the intentions that will come with the next cycle.

When the moon reaches its darkened phase, the quiet introspection of the new moon invites the practitioner to seek inner peace and realignment. In this phase, the practitioner can call upon Archangel Raphael, the angel of healing, to offer comfort and renewal. To create a tranquil space, the practitioner may light a single candle in an otherwise darkened room, allowing the glow to symbolize the hidden light within. Sitting in silence, they invite Archangel Raphael's healing presence to fill their mind and heart, connecting with the restorative energy of the new moon.

In this period, the practitioner can practice an angelic journaling exercise known as "Soul Planting," where they focus not on external goals but on the inner qualities they wish to nurture—peace, resilience, compassion, or forgiveness. By planting these seeds within the self, they align with the energies of renewal. With eyes closed, they visualize these qualities taking root within, beginning as small seeds and slowly growing into luminous blooms, nurtured by the quiet strength of the new moon.

As they move through each lunar cycle, the practitioner discovers that the consistent alignment with the moon and angelic presence brings a greater depth to their rituals. By engaging in specific practices during each phase, they grow attuned to the universal rhythms, feeling a strengthened connection with both the celestial cycles and the angelic realm. The practitioner learns to recognize the subtle differences in energy that each phase brings, becoming a vessel through which angelic guidance flows with ease.

The angels, too, respond with a heightened presence, their guidance shifting to align with the phase. During the waxing moon, messages might come in the form of encouragement, insights for growth, or symbols that inspire action. At the full moon, the angels may reveal deeper truths, bringing clarity to questions or situations, guiding the practitioner in moments of decision. During the waning moon, angelic guidance often focuses on release, forgiveness, and the gentle dissolution of attachments. And in the new moon's quiet, angels offer comfort, nurturing the spirit in preparation for the cycle's renewal.

By embracing the entirety of the lunar cycle, the practitioner transforms each phase into a sacred journey, one that deepens their awareness of divine presence in all things. The moon's rhythm becomes a reminder of the soul's ongoing cycles of growth, fulfillment, release, and renewal, mirroring the natural order in both the heavens and within. In following this path, the practitioner grows closer to the angels, who walk alongside them, guiding with compassion, understanding, and unwavering light. Through the dance of the moon and the communion with angels, life itself becomes a luminous cycle, ever-unfolding and filled with grace.

Chapter 19
Strengthening the Connection

Connection with angels can become a sustaining force in daily life, a quiet yet powerful presence that continually guides, protects, and inspires. Embracing practices that nurture this bond establishes a gentle rhythm that fosters spiritual closeness and strengthens sensitivity to angelic energies. Each day can hold moments for small, deliberate acts that allow one to tap into angelic support, weaving spiritual presence into the fabric of ordinary experience.

As one begins, the practice of setting an intention every morning becomes a doorway to connection. By simply pausing to acknowledge the day ahead and inviting angelic presence, the reader opens a pathway to guidance and alignment. Closing the eyes for a few moments, they breathe deeply, calling to mind the angel they feel closest to or simply addressing angels in general. This can be accompanied by a quiet phrase like, "Angels, walk with me today, bringing light to my thoughts and peace to my heart." This daily invocation aligns the practitioner with angelic energies, anchoring their focus on the values and strengths they hope to embody.

As the day unfolds, the practitioner can cultivate an awareness of angelic signs. The gentle nudge of intuition, a sudden feeling of peace amid stress, or the unexpected sighting of a symbol like a feather or a flash of light may serve as quiet reminders of angelic proximity. With each sign, the reader learns to recognize the subtle ways angels communicate, growing attuned to these cues. Taking a few moments to acknowledge each sign with gratitude reinforces the connection, as if responding to a friend's gesture with appreciation.

Another daily practice is the "light visualization." At any time, the reader can take a few seconds to imagine a warm light descending around them, wrapping them in an angelic embrace. This is a powerful way to shield oneself from negative influences and to establish a sense of calm and protection. Visualizing this light extending outward, the practitioner can also send this protective energy to loved ones or places that may need angelic blessing, building a habit of bringing light wherever it's most needed. This practice enhances both protection and compassion, as the reader becomes a channel of angelic energy for the world around them.

Nighttime offers a unique opportunity for reflection and reinforcement. Before sleep, the practitioner can engage in a ritual of review, closing their eyes and envisioning moments from the day. Where did they feel guided, safe, or uplifted? Where could they have embraced more peace or patience? This quiet introspection allows the reader to notice the angelic influence throughout their day, fostering gratitude and a deeper awareness of spiritual support. By visualizing angels standing close, perhaps near their bed, watching over them as they drift to sleep, they end the day wrapped in protection and love.

Beyond daily practices, creating a "sacred symbol" as a physical reminder of angelic connection can further strengthen this bond. This symbol could be a piece of jewelry, a crystal, or even a small decorative item, something that resonates with the individual's spiritual path. Every time they hold or see this symbol, they're reminded of the angels' presence in their life. Holding the symbol and repeating a silent affirmation like, "With this, I am always connected to my angels," serves as a powerful tool for reinforcing their bond, especially in moments of uncertainty or stress.

These simple yet profound daily acts lay the foundation for a continuous angelic presence. Each practice, like a bead on a string, weaves a strand of connection between the practitioner and the angelic realm. Through this awareness, angels are no longer occasional visitors but companions in each thought, feeling, and action. The gentle accumulation of these practices creates a life steeped in spiritual clarity, resilience, and guidance, transforming the everyday into a sacred journey shared with angels.

Deepening the daily connection with angels transforms simple practices into acts of reverence and strengthens the practitioner's bond to unseen guidance. Expanding upon initial connection rituals, additional practices encourage a more profound sense of spiritual presence and enhance the practitioner's sensitivity to angelic energies. With time and intention, these routines create a sustainable and enriching rhythm of angelic companionship.

In building consistency, the practitioner can begin with a simple morning and evening ritual that brings focus to each day's energy. Upon waking, they might sit quietly, focusing on steady breaths and imagining the gentle glow of angelic light filling their body and radiating outward. As they continue, they may silently repeat a mantra such as, "I am surrounded by light, and I walk with my angels." This grounding practice attunes the practitioner to angelic harmony before they encounter the day's unknowns, instilling a sense of calm, protection, and strength.

To reinforce this daily connection, practitioners can carry a "gratitude stone," a small, smooth stone or crystal infused with their intention to recognize blessings throughout the day. Each time they touch it, they take a brief moment to mentally note one source of gratitude, however small. This stone serves as a quiet reminder to notice angelic signs, and to maintain an openness to gentle, everyday guidance. Such touchstones are often more than symbols—they become conductors for connection, a reminder that angels accompany us even in ordinary moments.

Throughout the day, the practitioner can strengthen their connection by embracing mindful actions, observing each experience with curiosity, as though witnessing an unfolding message from their angels. If they encounter a sense of guidance or intuition, they pause to note it without judgment. Angels often communicate through these subtle impressions, and by practicing non-attachment, the reader learns to trust intuitive responses and gentle cues. This mindful state sharpens their perception and allows them to notice angelic guidance that otherwise might pass unnoticed.

As the evening draws close, a deeper practice of reflection takes place. Here, the practitioner returns to a quiet space, ideally near their altar or another serene setting, and reviews the events of the day. This reflection is more than a recounting—it's an examination of moments when they sensed the angels' influence. They may ask, "Where did I feel led toward peace, patience, or understanding?" or "Where could I have opened myself more fully to angelic guidance?" This exercise strengthens self-awareness and trust, helping the practitioner learn from angelic teachings embedded in daily life.

To deepen this connection further, the practitioner can create a "ritual of release" before sleep, mentally releasing any lingering emotions or worries from the day. In a calm state, they imagine these worries as clouds gently drifting away, watched over by angels who guide them toward healing. With this, they practice surrender, an acknowledgment that angels protect and nurture even in the unseen realms of dreams and sleep. As they drift into slumber, they might visualize a circle of light around them, a quiet assurance of safety and peace.

A further element of deepening connection lies in affirmations that bridge the conscious and subconscious. The practitioner can develop personalized affirmations that reflect their intent to grow closer to their angels. Simple phrases like "I trust in angelic guidance," "I am open to spiritual wisdom," or "I walk with grace and protection" become declarations of faith and intent. Repeating these affirmations during moments of quiet, or writing them in a journal, sets a foundation for spiritual alignment, even amid life's unpredictability.

For those who seek a more vivid sense of angelic presence, practicing focused visualization exercises can be transformative. They may visualize themselves walking alongside their guardian angel or bathed in a radiant light that expands and protects. These practices deepen spiritual sensitivity, fostering a heightened sense of peace and assurance that angels accompany each step. Practiced regularly, visualization becomes a powerful method to reinforce angelic proximity and strengthen the practitioner's inner sanctuary.

The final layer of strengthening the connection lies in acts of service, bringing the angels' values into the world through kindness, compassion, and understanding. When one helps another, offers kindness, or responds to difficulty with grace, they bring angelic qualities into action. This lived expression of angelic presence amplifies their connection, as their actions echo the compassionate guidance of angels. With time, they learn that angelic energy exists not only in moments of meditation and ritual but in how they engage the world.

Through these deepening practices, the reader begins to experience angelic presence as a steady, consistent element in their life. Each act, whether of gratitude, intention, visualization, or kindness, weaves a thread that binds them closer to the angelic realm. In return, they may feel a growing sense of peace, protection, and resilience—a life shared with angels, nourished by small but profound acts of connection.

Chapter 20
Connecting with the Personal Guardian Angel

Beyond general angelic presences, each person is believed to walk through life with a unique guardian angel—a constant, silent companion attuned specifically to their path and purpose. Guidance here opens a door to that deeper connection, offering exercises to cultivate a conscious relationship with their personal guardian angel, fostering trust and familiarity with this being of light.

As the practitioner embarks on this connection, the first step is to create a tranquil space where they can turn inward without distraction. They may light a candle and focus on its gentle glow, imagining that this light represents the pure presence of their guardian angel. With closed eyes, they might take deep breaths, visualizing a stream of radiant, golden light filling their heart and expanding outward, creating a warm sphere of energy around them. This act of focus, enveloped in light, sets the stage for the subtle connection.

Once in this state of peace, the practitioner begins to call upon their guardian angel with sincerity, using words that reflect their unique relationship. They might say, "Beloved guardian angel, I invite your presence here and open my heart to receive your light and guidance." In time, these words need no speaking; the intent itself becomes a whisper in the soul, a gentle invitation that calls forth a connection beyond words.

As they hold this quiet focus, a sense of familiarity or a subtle feeling of warmth may arise, as though enveloped in a protective embrace. The practitioner is encouraged to be patient and receptive, noticing any sensations or impressions, however faint they may be. For some, there may be a feeling of peaceful presence, while others might experience a soft wave of energy or even see a fleeting image of light in their mind's eye. These sensations become part of the practitioner's growing awareness, each connection deepening their bond with their guardian angel.

Over time, to further solidify this bond, the practitioner can engage in a practice called "soul dialogue," which involves mentally posing questions and listening for a response from within. They might begin with gentle, open-ended questions, such as "What wisdom do you have for me today?" or "How can I better align with my purpose?" While the answers might not be immediate or loud, a faint impression, thought, or feeling often arises, providing guidance that seems to speak softly to the heart.

Another technique for strengthening this relationship is the practice of journaling as if the guardian angel were speaking through the words. The practitioner can write out a question, then allow their hand to move freely as thoughts, words, or feelings flow onto the page. Over time, patterns and phrases emerge, helping the practitioner distinguish their guardian angel's gentle guidance from their own mind's chatter. This "written conversation" becomes a tangible way to build trust and understand the voice of their guardian angel.

The practitioner may also create a "guardian angel token," a personal item imbued with their intention to connect. This token could be a small crystal, a feather, or another object that holds special meaning. When held or placed nearby, it serves as a physical reminder of their guardian angel's presence and support, helping them feel grounded in the knowledge that they are never alone. Over time, this simple item becomes a cherished symbol, a bridge between the physical and spiritual realms.

With practice, the practitioner becomes more attuned to recognizing signs of their guardian angel's presence beyond the confines of ritual. They might notice synchronicities, such as timely encounters, patterns in nature, or a sudden feeling of calm in moments of uncertainty. These subtle signs serve as gentle affirmations, reminders that the guardian angel is actively involved, guiding, and watching over them. The more the practitioner acknowledges these signs, the clearer and more frequent they become, as if the guardian angel's presence becomes woven into the fabric of daily life.

A final practice for deepening this connection is learning to feel the guardian angel's presence in moments of solitude. The practitioner may set aside time to sit quietly, not with a mind focused on questions or requests, but in simple companionship. They close their eyes, breathe deeply, and simply rest in awareness, letting themselves feel enveloped in warmth and peace. In these moments, they come to understand their guardian angel's presence as a loyal companion, always present in the background, waiting with patience and love.

Through these practices, the connection with the guardian angel matures from mere concept to living relationship. Over time, the practitioner discovers that this bond is not just a comforting thought but a profound support, an ever-present force that steadies and guides them through life's journey. By building trust, engaging in dialogue, and recognizing signs, they bring their guardian angel closer, creating a relationship that is felt in the heart and known in the soul.

The relationship with a guardian angel deepens as the practitioner learns to receive guidance through intuitive channels, establishing a bond that becomes a powerful source of comfort, wisdom, and support in moments of need. Building on the practices of invitation and recognition, additional guidance introduces ways to cultivate and interpret the intuitive impressions and signs that arise from this angelic connection.

To enhance receptivity to their guardian angel, the practitioner begins by refining their alignment of mind and heart. This alignment is essential to clear the mental "static" that can cloud perception, allowing guidance to emerge with greater clarity. The practitioner may start with a simple breathing technique: placing their hand on their heart and taking slow, deliberate breaths, feeling a rhythm of inner calm. They visualize a flow of light moving through their body, relaxing each muscle, releasing tension, and preparing the mind to rest in openness. This state of calm invites a gentle, receptive energy, clearing the way for intuitive impressions to surface.

Once this foundation of calm is set, the practitioner engages in focused listening, often called "inner listening," where they pose a specific question or request for guidance. This question might be as simple as, "Please show me the path forward," or "What is the wisdom you wish to share with me today?" Following this request, they enter a period of stillness, not expecting an immediate answer but allowing thoughts, images, or feelings to arise naturally. The impressions received may be subtle—a sensation, a word, or an image that appears spontaneously in the mind's eye.

Over time, the practitioner begins to recognize the ways their guardian angel communicates uniquely with them. Some may find that their angelic guidance comes as flashes of insight or images that hold symbolic meaning, while others might feel a physical sensation of warmth or tingling that signals their angel's response. Through practice, the practitioner learns to trust these personal "signatures" of communication, discerning when a thought or feeling is influenced by the guardian angel's presence.

One technique for interpreting these impressions is to keep a dedicated journal of angelic communication. After each session of inner listening, the practitioner records the thoughts, images, or feelings that surfaced, even if they seem ambiguous or fragmentary. Reviewing these entries over time reveals patterns, recurrent symbols, or messages that form a cohesive language of guidance. This journal becomes a treasured resource, a personal record of the dialogue with the guardian angel, offering both insight and comfort.

In addition to inner listening, the practitioner learns to seek guidance through signs and synchronicities in their environment. By setting an intention to receive a sign from their guardian angel, they open their awareness to subtle cues in the world around them. This might take the form of specific numbers, like seeing "111" or "444" repeatedly, a song with relevant lyrics playing unexpectedly, or a timely conversation that addresses a concern or question on their heart. These synchronicities serve as gentle nudges, affirming that their guardian angel is present, attentive, and responsive.

In moments of decision-making, the practitioner can call on their guardian angel's guidance to support clarity and confidence. They may start by framing a specific question and inviting the angel's insight. Afterward, the practitioner pays attention to any internal shift or sense of peace that may arise when contemplating one option over another. Often, the guidance from the guardian angel is felt as a quiet yet profound sense of "rightness," as if the chosen path resonates deeply within the soul, bringing both assurance and relief.

As the practitioner becomes more adept at sensing their guardian angel's presence, they may seek to incorporate this relationship into their daily routines, inviting the angel's guidance in both mundane and spiritual tasks. From small requests for patience in traffic to moments of inspiration before a creative endeavor, these brief interactions weave the guardian angel's influence throughout their daily life. In time, the practitioner realizes that their angel is not just a presence for times of ritual or meditation but a constant companion, present in every aspect of life.

Another practice for deepening the connection is setting aside moments each day to express gratitude for the guidance and protection received. This expression of thanks may be as simple as a heartfelt thought or a brief prayer acknowledging the angel's influence and care. In giving thanks, the practitioner strengthens the energy of love and trust between themselves and their guardian angel, creating a bond that resonates more deeply with each acknowledgment.

Through these practices, the practitioner finds themselves growing in intuition, inner strength, and spiritual insight, rooted in the assurance that they are never alone. The relationship with their guardian angel becomes a wellspring of wisdom and guidance that nurtures their path, offering clarity in uncertainty, strength in challenge, and unwavering companionship in solitude. As they walk their path with the presence of this celestial guide, life itself feels transformed, as though seen through a lens of light, connection, and trust.

Chapter 21
Angelic Protection for Home and Family

To invite angelic protection into the home and safeguard loved ones, the practitioner learns to perform rituals and intentional acts that align their living space with angelic presence. These practices call upon the guardian angels not only of the individual but of the home itself—a space that holds the energy and well-being of those within it. Various methods strengthen the protection and harmony of the home, turning it into a sanctuary of peace, love, and spiritual resilience.

The process begins by dedicating time to clear and harmonize the environment. Clutter and stagnant energy are believed to disrupt spiritual flow, so a careful physical and energetic cleansing of each room is a vital step. The practitioner starts by opening windows and doors to invite fresh air and new energy, visualizing light sweeping through the rooms, corners, and doorways. This act of physical cleaning becomes the foundation upon which angelic presence can be invited to rest more fully.

With the home physically prepared, the practitioner selects elements for protection that resonate with the energy of angels. Items like candles, crystals, and specific herbs are carefully chosen and placed around the home. Candles are often used as symbols of light; lighting one with intention at a central location within the house—perhaps an altar or a protected corner—serves as a beacon to attract protective energies. White candles, in particular, are revered for purity and peace, inviting the watchful eyes of angels to surround the space.

Crystals such as black tourmaline, selenite, and amethyst are positioned in key areas to maintain an atmosphere of balance and protection. Black tourmaline near entryways can absorb any dense or negative energy before it enters, while selenite near windows allows gentle, cleansing vibrations to flow in. Amethyst, placed in living rooms or family gathering spaces, cultivates a feeling of harmony and calm, creating an aura of spiritual protection.

Herbs such as rosemary and sage further enhance the protective shield. The practitioner may use sage or palo santo to "smudge" each room, allowing the smoke to clear lingering energies, particularly in spaces where stress, illness, or conflict have occurred. This act of smoke cleansing purifies, creating a new space for positive angelic forces. After smudging, placing a small bundle of rosemary or bay leaves near the main door is believed to guard the home against negativity, while lavender promotes serenity, warding off discord and inviting peace.

Once the space is prepared and harmonized, the practitioner invites angelic protection with an invocation, spoken with reverence and intention. A simple prayer might go as follows: "Angels of light, I invite your presence here. Guard this home and all within, surround us with love and light, and let this place be a haven of peace and protection." As these words are spoken, the practitioner visualizes a glowing sphere of light around the home, growing stronger and more vibrant with each word. This sphere is imagined as a protective boundary, sheltering the family within from any external negativity or harm.

At times when family members are in need of special protection—such as during illness, travels, or life transitions—the practitioner may invoke the guardian angels of each person, naming them individually and entrusting them to the angels' care. This act of specific invocation reinforces the unique support each family member receives, cultivating a feeling of unity and comfort. The practitioner can extend this protective energy by visualizing each person enveloped in a soft, shimmering light, a cocoon of angelic presence accompanying them wherever they go.

Family symbols, such as shared objects or meaningful heirlooms, can also be blessed with angelic energy and placed at the center of the home. These objects hold the spirit of the family's unity and love, acting as energetic anchors that bond the home's occupants to one another and to the protective energies around them. A small ritual can be performed in which each person touches the object, symbolizing their connection to one another and to the blessing that surrounds them.

Regular renewal of this protective intention is encouraged, reinforcing the energy over time. Some choose to repeat these protective practices each month, aligning with the phases of the moon for added potency. Others may choose specific times, such as dawn or dusk, to repeat the invocation, lighting a candle and reaffirming the boundary of angelic presence around the home. This ritual consistency deepens the protective connection, forming a lasting spiritual framework within the home.

Recognizing angelic presence within the home is a gentle practice of attunement. Often, it is subtle—a sudden sense of peace, a delicate warmth in the air, or an unexpected moment of calm amid family life. These quiet moments are reminders of the angels' presence, reassuring the practitioner that their home remains protected and held within an angelic sphere. Noticing these signs can become part of daily life, a constant reminder of divine guardianship and the sanctuary the angels help create.

In times of distress or need, the practitioner calls upon this protective network, knowing the home is more than mere walls and rooms—it is a sanctuary touched by angelic grace. The boundaries created are spiritual, yet their effects are felt tangibly. The energy within the home becomes one of comfort, safety, and light, a place where each family member feels secure, loved, and held. The rituals deepen a connection with angels that goes beyond protection, weaving a fabric of love and unity that strengthens both home and heart.

The ongoing protection of a home is a layered and living practice, meant to grow and adapt with the family it guards. Angelic protection deepens over time, offering a reservoir of strength and peace during both everyday moments and times of transition. Guidance on reinforcing this bond of protection expands upon previously introduced rituals to create a sustained relationship with angelic guardianship.

In moments of significant transition, such as a move, a new beginning, or a family celebration, the energy within the home naturally shifts, creating opportunities to refresh and empower its spiritual shield. During these times, the practitioner may conduct a dedicated ritual to call upon angelic protection. In preparing for this ritual, the practitioner first considers the atmosphere of the home, fostering an environment that aligns with their intention. They begin by cleansing the space, either through smudging with sage or another cleansing herb, or through sound—bells, chimes, or gentle chanting are all effective ways to clear stagnant energies and make space for renewal.

At the heart of this expanded protection ritual lies the establishment of a connection with the specific energies of archangels traditionally associated with home protection. Archangel Michael, known as the protector and guide, is often called upon for strength, resilience, and the courage to face challenges. Archangel Raphael, the angel of healing, brings harmony, ensuring that the emotional and spiritual health of the family remains fortified. Invoking these archangels creates a feeling of structured strength and reassurance, as if a canopy of protection has been placed over the home.

The invocation may be personalized, but a simple example could be: "Archangel Michael, guardian of peace and protection, we invite you to watch over our home and keep us safe from all harm. Archangel Raphael, angel of healing, infuse this space with balance and tranquility, filling our home with love and health." As the practitioner speaks, they visualize each archangel's energy filling the home. Michael's presence might be felt as a strong, protective light encircling the home's boundaries, while

Raphael's is often perceived as a gentle, green light infusing the rooms with healing energy.

To anchor this protective presence in the physical realm, symbols of the archangels—such as small statues, stones, or candles—can be placed at key locations around the home, particularly near doors and windows. These symbols act as reminders of the archangels' presence and provide a tangible link to their protective influence. At the main entrance, the practitioner may place a small amulet or stone blessed with the intention of protection, such as black tourmaline or hematite, to reinforce the threshold as a barrier against negativity.

In times of conflict or stress within the home, the practitioner may draw upon this connection to seek immediate angelic assistance. Inviting the angels' calming presence into tense situations can transform the energy within moments. This is done simply by pausing, taking a deep breath, and asking for angelic guidance, either silently or aloud. Phrases such as "Angels of peace, bring harmony to this place," or "Archangel Raphael, restore balance here," act as gentle yet powerful calls for assistance. The practitioner may even visualize a soft light descending upon those present, washing away tension and bringing comfort.

As an ongoing practice, weekly or monthly rituals help renew the energy of angelic protection, much like tending to a garden. Each renewal ritual does not have to be lengthy; lighting a candle, saying a short prayer, or taking a few minutes to silently invoke angelic presence can all serve to fortify the protective energies already in place. With each repetition, the practitioner's connection to this protective force grows stronger, and the energy of the home becomes increasingly attuned to angelic frequencies.

Understanding and clearing dense energies is another essential aspect of ongoing protection. Over time, even in a spiritually fortified space, energies from daily stresses, emotional upheavals, or external influences may collect and create a feeling of heaviness. In these cases, the practitioner can use a more intensive cleansing ritual, combining smudging, sound, and visualizations to sweep the home free of stagnant energy. They may envision the angels walking through each room, their light expanding and dissolving any lingering darkness.

Another effective method of dispelling dense energy involves creating a "light grid" within the home. The practitioner can place small crystals—such as clear quartz or selenite—at each corner of a room or throughout the home. This grid acts as a conduit for angelic energy, maintaining a steady flow of protection and purity. The practitioner can then invoke the angels, asking them to activate and bless this grid, allowing it to serve as an ongoing barrier against unwanted energies.

An essential component of this sustained connection to angelic guardianship is the practice of gratitude. Regularly expressing thanks for the angels' presence in the home deepens the relationship, making the space more receptive to their ongoing protection. Simple moments of gratitude—such as silently thanking the angels while lighting a candle or leaving a flower as an offering on the altar—reinforce the protective link. This gratitude becomes a cycle of mutual respect, with the home itself becoming more attuned to the harmony and love of angelic protection.

As the relationship between the practitioner and angelic forces matures, a more intuitive bond develops. The practitioner may begin to sense subtle shifts in the home's atmosphere, instinctively feeling when to call upon the angels' presence more strongly or when to offer thanks. Signs of this intuitive connection often manifest as gentle warmth, a fleeting sparkle of light, or a sense of peace that appears in moments of need. These signs are reminders that the angels' watchful presence remains active, wrapping the home and its inhabitants in a soft yet powerful embrace.

In embracing these rituals and practices, the practitioner transforms the home into a sanctuary. The structure itself becomes imbued with light, each wall and room holding the echoes of prayers, invocations, and angelic visits. The family dwelling becomes a space where both spirit and heart find refuge, creating a legacy of protection that is felt by all who enter. This angelic guardianship offers more than just security; it serves as a profound reminder of the invisible support that surrounds and sustains, a timeless shelter of love that the family carries forward, day by day.

Chapter 22
The Role of Archangels in Rituals

Within the vast hierarchy of angelic beings, the archangels stand as pillars of celestial strength, wisdom, and power. They carry distinct energies and preside over areas of life that resonate deeply with human experiences—protection, healing, transformation, and divine communication. To invite the presence of archangels into a ritual is to call upon forces capable of profoundly influencing both the spiritual and material realms.

Each archangel embodies a unique purpose and specialization, offering guidance and support that aligns with specific human needs. Among these exalted beings, Archangel Michael is perhaps the most frequently invoked. As the archangel of protection and courage, he is often visualized wielding a powerful sword of light, which cuts through fear and negativity. Michael's presence can be felt as a wave of strength and reassurance, enveloping those who call upon him with an aura of indomitable protection. Rituals that invoke Michael are ideal for moments when the practitioner seeks resilience against life's challenges or desires a shield against negative forces.

Archangel Raphael, whose name means "God heals," is another prominent figure within angelic rituals. Known as the angel of healing, Raphael's energy is soft yet pervasive, bringing a nurturing presence to those in need of physical, emotional, or spiritual restoration. When invoking Raphael, the practitioner may envision a green, soothing light that flows through and around them, dissolving pain, and encouraging the body and mind to align with a state of health and wholeness. Raphael's presence is especially helpful in rituals centered on recovery, self-love, and renewal, as his energy enhances the natural healing capacities within.

In matters of communication and divine wisdom, Archangel Gabriel shines as a guide and messenger. Often associated with clarity and creative inspiration, Gabriel's presence opens channels for authentic expression and insight. Gabriel's energy is powerful yet gentle, carrying messages from the higher realms to aid in understanding and foresight. In rituals that seek guidance, vision, or support in creative pursuits, Gabriel's influence acts as a bridge between the practitioner's aspirations and the insights needed to manifest them. When invoking Gabriel, one might visualize a pure, white light that illuminates the path ahead, encouraging confidence and conviction in their voice and choices.

Each invocation to an archangel begins with reverence, for to call upon such high beings is to open oneself to their immense energy. As the ritual begins, the practitioner may light a candle, offering its flame as a beacon to invite the angel's presence. Facing each archangel's direction—Michael to the south, Raphael to the east, Gabriel to the west, and Uriel to the north—strengthens the invocation, aligning it with both earthly and cosmic energies. Speaking directly to the archangel, the practitioner vocalizes their intention, for clarity of purpose amplifies the connection.

The invocation of Archangel Uriel brings yet another dimension to angelic rituals, especially those focused on wisdom and inner light. Uriel's name means "God is my light," and he is often called upon in moments of decision-making or when clarity and wisdom are needed. Uriel's energy can be felt as a grounding force, often visualized as a deep, golden light that illuminates the mind and clears away confusion. He is a gentle yet firm presence, bringing knowledge, clarity, and insight that cut through doubt. In Uriel's presence, answers seem to surface with ease, as if emerging from the depths of the subconscious. His role in guiding and enlightening makes Uriel an ideal companion for rituals centered on wisdom, study, and problem-solving.

The power of invoking an archangel is intensified through the use of sacred symbols or words unique to each angel. In calling upon Michael, the practitioner may choose to draw or visualize the symbol of a sword or shield, evoking his protective strength. For Raphael, a green healing light or a small crystal, like aventurine or malachite, resonates with his energy. Gabriel's symbol may be that of a trumpet or a flowing water symbol, representing the fluidity of communication and divine guidance. For Uriel, visualizing a radiant sun or a piece of amber connects to his enlightening energy, grounding the practitioner in wisdom.

In rituals that include the archangels, the practitioner enters a space not just of personal reflection but of communion with the higher realms. Each archangel brings a piece of the divine essence into the sacred space, creating a potent environment where transformation and growth can flourish. The practitioner may feel a tangible shift as each archangel's energy surrounds them—a warm, safe, and uplifting presence that seems to expand beyond the boundaries of the room.

As the ritual progresses, the practitioner may find themselves engaging in a silent dialogue with the archangels. Questions arise naturally, not always spoken aloud, yet answers seem to flow intuitively, as if the heart were listening directly to angelic wisdom. In this state, each archangel's guidance can feel as though it moves through the soul itself, touching parts of the spirit where healing, courage, clarity, or wisdom are needed most.

After receiving the archangels' energies, it is essential to offer thanks, acknowledging the sacred bond shared during the ritual. A gesture of gratitude—whether through words, a simple bow, or an offering such as flowers or incense—deepens the connection, honoring the presence of these celestial beings. By expressing this gratitude, the practitioner strengthens the bond, ensuring that the connection remains open and receptive in future times of need.

The presence of archangels in rituals carries lasting effects. Often, practitioners report a sense of inner strength, clarity, or healing that lingers well beyond the ritual's end. This connection, once established, can be revisited in times of reflection or in daily moments when support is needed. In forming relationships with these angelic guides, the practitioner nurtures a living bridge between the earthly and the divine, one that grows stronger and more profound with each invocation.

In the days following the ritual, the practitioner may continue to feel the subtle influence of the archangels. Moments of clarity, strength, or peace may arise unexpectedly, as though the angels are nearby, offering a gentle reminder of their presence. This lingering connection acts as both a shield and a guide, protecting and supporting the practitioner on their path. By inviting the archangels into their life, the practitioner walks forward with the assurance that they are not alone but journeying in communion with beings who reflect the divine light within.

The power of invoking archangels deepens as practitioners grow more attuned to their unique energies, allowing for a more nuanced and intentional connection. Each archangel, though constant in essence, responds dynamically to the needs of the moment, bringing guidance and clarity suited to the practitioner's specific spiritual growth. In this way, invoking archangels is not merely an act of petition but becomes a profound collaboration between human and celestial realms. With practice, this communion evolves, enabling a richer experience and understanding of angelic wisdom.

Each archangel's energy has a rhythm, a frequency that can be sensed and harmonized with. To intensify this connection, practitioners employ visualization techniques and rituals that act as conduits, amplifying their presence. For instance, invoking Archangel Michael becomes more potent when the practitioner creates an image of themselves surrounded by his protective blue flame, a shield that stands against any negativity or fear. With intention and breath, the practitioner envisions this flame encircling them, expanding with each inhalation. A heightened sense of security fills the space, and the practitioner feels anchored, empowered by Michael's unwavering strength.

Archangel Raphael's energy manifests through the soft vibrations of green light, a color long associated with healing and renewal. In deepening the connection with Raphael, practitioners often integrate the element of touch—placing hands over the heart or on areas in need of healing while visualizing Raphael's green light permeating these spaces. With each visualization, the green light pulses, invigorating cells and harmonizing the mind, body, and spirit. In this state of calm receptivity, Raphael's guidance can be more easily perceived as subtle thoughts or gentle nudges, steering the practitioner toward choices and practices that nurture well-being.

When calling upon Archangel Gabriel, practitioners find a guiding light in the archangel's association with clarity, purpose, and expression. Gabriel's energy moves fluidly, like water, encouraging communication and creativity. To amplify this connection, a simple yet potent ritual involves lighting a white candle—symbolizing purity and insight—and offering a few moments of silent intention, inviting Gabriel's guidance in matters of self-expression or decision-making. The practitioner may place a clear quartz crystal nearby, which helps to refine Gabriel's messages, bringing clarity to their thoughts or projects. This ritual acts as a beacon, inviting Gabriel's presence and creating an open pathway for inspiration to flow, especially useful when one feels creatively blocked or uncertain.

Archangel Uriel, the bearer of wisdom and illumination, calls forth a connection that resonates with stability and clarity. Practitioners seeking Uriel's guidance find that grounding exercises help prepare for his presence. Standing barefoot on the earth or visualizing roots extending from the feet into the ground can help establish this connection, bringing Uriel's steadying energy into the body. Uriel's golden light, seen as a source of inner enlightenment, fills the practitioner's mind, lifting the fog of doubt and providing answers that arise not as instructions but as a deep inner knowing. By communing with Uriel, the practitioner cultivates a grounded clarity, an awareness that serves as an unwavering compass.

In a more advanced invocation, practitioners may call upon multiple archangels in a single ritual, each aligned with a particular direction—Michael in the south, Gabriel in the west, Raphael in the east, and Uriel in the north. Standing at the center of this circle, the practitioner becomes enveloped by the archangels' combined energies, each complementing the other to create a balanced field of protection, healing, wisdom, and guidance. This harmonious convergence creates a fortified sanctuary, a space where the practitioner feels secure yet deeply connected to the divine. As each archangel is acknowledged in their respective direction, the ritual gains depth, bringing a sense of unity and alignment between the practitioner and the archangels.

As the connection with the archangels strengthens, the practitioner may begin to notice that their guidance appears in daily life through synchronicities, symbols, or subtle shifts in perception. The archangels communicate not solely through the direct channels of meditation or ritual but through the language of signs—numbers, feathers, or even unexpected interactions that carry a message. Archangel Michael's presence may be felt as an increased sense of courage during challenges; Raphael's as a peaceful, healing energy that lingers after illness or stress; Gabriel's as newfound clarity in conversations; and Uriel's as sudden insights that illuminate decisions. These experiences reinforce the practitioner's bond with the archangels, transforming the practice from ritual to an ongoing relationship.

Closing a ritual with the archangels is as vital as the invocation itself, serving as an honoring of the presence and energy each archangel has provided. A final moment of gratitude—whether through a verbal expression, a gesture, or a simple thought—allows the practitioner to gently release the energies invoked, ensuring a harmonious return to the earthly plane. This respectful closing also signals the practitioner's readiness to carry forward the insights gained, integrating them into their day-to-day life. The gratitude expressed in this closure resonates as a blessing, reinforcing the bond and leaving a residual sense of the archangels' presence.

By engaging deeply with the archangels through ritual, the practitioner fosters a unique and evolving connection with each. The archangels, though transcendent, respond to this intentional relationship with attentiveness, guiding the practitioner through life's complexities with wisdom, protection, and grace.

Chapter 23
Channeling Messages

The practice of channeling messages from angels invites the practitioner to explore a state of heightened spiritual receptivity, allowing subtle insights and angelic wisdom to flow into consciousness. Channeling is both an art and a spiritual discipline, grounded in trust and openness. In this state, the practitioner surrenders mental noise and daily distractions, attuning instead to the finer frequencies of angelic communication. Channeling does not seek to control or anticipate messages; it is a practice of allowing, of creating a receptive vessel within which angelic messages can be received and honored.

As the practitioner enters this receptive state, calm and grounded breathing serves as the bridge to the spiritual realms. The breath, slow and intentional, clears the mind and prepares the body for the gentle energies of angelic communication. Each inhalation draws in a sense of peace and connection, while each exhalation releases tension and worldly concerns. As the breath becomes rhythmically slow, a natural calm arises, creating space for channeling to begin. In this place of inner quiet, the practitioner's spirit feels more aligned with the angelic frequencies, receptive to impressions and whispers of guidance.

To initiate the channeling process, the practitioner may begin with a brief invocation or prayer, inviting their guardian angel or a specific archangel into the space. This invitation is made with respect and humility, acknowledging the angel's presence as a sacred gift. With eyes closed or gently focused on a candle flame, the practitioner holds an open question in their heart—something simple and sincere, reflecting a true need for clarity or wisdom. This question acts as a point of resonance, helping the angel attune their guidance to the practitioner's intentions. Yet the practitioner remains unattached to specific answers, trusting that what arises will align with the greater good.

The messages themselves may come in various forms—words, images, sensations, or even colors that carry symbolic meaning. Often, the first impressions are subtle, almost like whispers within the mind or glimpses of thought that appear effortlessly. Trusting these initial impressions is essential, as angels often communicate through the language of intuition rather than overt messages. A single word, a symbol, or even a feeling of warmth may convey layers of meaning that unfold as the practitioner reflects on them. The key is not to analyze in the moment but to simply receive and observe, allowing the messages to flow unimpeded.

To aid memory and reflection, the practitioner keeps a journal nearby, ready to record the impressions received. Writing immediately after a channeling session captures the essence of the message before the conscious mind intervenes. Each word or symbol noted serves as a bridge to deeper understanding, and over time, patterns emerge. A journal entry may start as a single phrase—"Trust the path"—but later insights may expand this into a meaningful reminder during times of doubt. These messages, often simple yet profound, form a thread of angelic wisdom that guides the practitioner's life and decisions.

With practice, the practitioner begins to sense when a message resonates as genuinely angelic versus when it may stem from personal thought or expectation. Angelic messages typically carry a tone of calm clarity and resonate with love, compassion, and encouragement. They may gently challenge the practitioner to grow but will never evoke fear or urgency. In contrast, mental chatter often feels fragmented, rushing with urgency or laden with judgment. Developing this discernment strengthens the practitioner's confidence in channeling, helping them recognize the authentic, unwavering presence of angelic guidance.

Certain practices can deepen the accuracy of channeling. Using crystals such as amethyst or celestite can amplify spiritual receptivity, creating an atmosphere of calm and clarity conducive to angelic communication. Placing the crystal nearby or holding it during meditation can help the practitioner tune into higher frequencies. Additionally, music with soothing tones or gentle chimes can aid in elevating the practitioner's energy, enhancing focus and maintaining a relaxed, open state. These elements are not necessary but can serve as helpful allies, creating a sacred environment for channeling.

As the practitioner's relationship with channeling evolves, they may choose to call upon specific angels for guidance in particular areas of life. For instance, when seeking clarity in relationships, Archangel Chamuel's compassionate energy may offer insights into understanding and harmony. When confronting personal challenges, invoking Archangel Michael brings courage and inner strength. Each archangel brings a unique quality to the session, aligning the guidance with the practitioner's specific needs and reinforcing their connection to the angelic realms.

Occasionally, the practitioner may experience moments of profound communion, where the presence of the angel feels almost tangible—a comforting warmth, a gentle touch, or a feeling of immense peace. These moments, though rare, confirm the reality of angelic connection and inspire a deep sense of gratitude. Such experiences, however fleeting, leave an imprint of peace and assurance, strengthening the practitioner's commitment to channeling and to honoring the guidance received.

Closing a channeling session is as meaningful as opening it. The practitioner offers gratitude, recognizing the angel's presence and guidance, regardless of the clarity or amount of information received. Gratitude forms a bridge of continuity, a reminder that the relationship with the angelic realm is ongoing and accessible. By closing with a simple blessing or acknowledgment, the practitioner signals respect for the energies invited and a willingness to integrate the messages received with integrity.

In embracing the art of channeling, the practitioner becomes a vessel for angelic wisdom, receiving messages that resonate beyond the personal and touch upon universal truths. These messages, often gentle reminders of peace, courage, or compassion, weave into the practitioner's daily life, influencing their choices, perceptions, and relationships. The journey of channeling unfolds as a path of deepening trust, where the practitioner learns to listen not only with the mind but with the heart, opening a gateway for angelic presence to transform and uplift their life.

The journey of channeling messages from angels delves deeper into refining perception, honing discernment, and embracing a state of openness where messages can unfold with clarity and authenticity. Channeling is an exercise in trust, requiring the practitioner to relinquish control over the process and allow the gentle, unfiltered presence of the angelic realm to permeate consciousness. As the practice deepens, so does the ability to interpret and distinguish genuine angelic guidance from one's own internal dialogue, strengthening the bond between the practitioner and the angelic realms.

To deepen the practice of channeling, the practitioner can begin by creating a more focused space for communication. An intentional space, perhaps adorned with angelic symbols or comforting light, serves as a spiritual anchor, easing the practitioner into a relaxed state where messages are more likely to emerge clearly. In this space, a comfortable seat and a calm setting enhance the ability to stay open without distraction. This intentionality signals to the angels that the practitioner is prepared, attentive, and respectful, opening the channel of communication with reverence.

As the practitioner settles, they might enter a focused breathing pattern, known as resonant or rhythmic breathing. Breathing in to a count of four, holding gently, and releasing to a similar count harmonizes the body and mind, easing both into a receptive state. This rhythm invites subtle energy into alignment, allowing a balanced flow of communication. As thoughts drift in, they are acknowledged without attachment, keeping the mind calm and centered. Gradually, this rhythm creates a soft barrier against distractions, so the practitioner's awareness becomes increasingly attuned to angelic frequencies.

Visualizations can further aid in refining this state. A visualization of light descending from above, enveloping the practitioner, can act as a medium through which messages flow. In this visualization, the light grows with each breath, surrounding and filling the practitioner, creating a bridge between earthly awareness and the angelic realm. This image of a luminous connection fosters trust, helping to ease any mental resistance that might block messages. The light serves as both protector and amplifier, strengthening clarity and openness as the practitioner sinks deeper into the channeling state.

Once the practitioner feels centered, they may set a focused intention for the session, framing an open-ended question to guide the channeling process. Questions such as "What wisdom can I receive for this stage of my life?" or "What insights do the angels wish to share?" invite the angelic realm to offer guidance without constraints. The practitioner then quiets the mind, trusting that whatever appears—be it words, images, or even subtle sensations—carries purpose. Releasing expectations about the format or timing of the message allows for a flow that feels spontaneous and genuine.

As impressions emerge, the practitioner becomes attuned to differentiating between angelic guidance and personal thoughts. Angelic messages are often gentle yet profound, sometimes evoking emotions of peace or joy. Personal thoughts, in contrast, may feel more directive or analytical. To aid in discernment, the practitioner may also rely on physical cues, such as a subtle sense of warmth or tingling, that often accompanies angelic presence. Practicing this discernment regularly sharpens intuition, enabling the practitioner to feel confident in recognizing authentic messages.

Over time, patterns may emerge within these messages—common themes, recurring symbols, or a particular angelic voice that seems to resonate. This sense of consistency and continuity strengthens the practitioner's relationship with specific angels. For instance, a practitioner may notice that Archangel Raphael's guidance often comes with images of green light or sensations of warmth when addressing matters of healing, while Michael's presence might be accompanied by feelings of strength and courage. Recognizing these patterns creates a personal "language" of angelic symbols and signs that becomes more intuitive with time.

Recording each session immediately afterward is essential, capturing even the smallest details before they fade. The practitioner may feel called to write freely, capturing impressions without worrying about structure or interpretation at first. Upon reviewing these entries over weeks or months, a deeper understanding of angelic guidance may reveal itself. Insights that initially seemed minor or vague often take on new meaning in hindsight, revealing layers of wisdom that align with the practitioner's unfolding life experiences.

Advanced practices in channeling may also involve specific techniques to strengthen communication. Chanting a mantra or angelic name, such as "Michael," "Gabriel," or "Raphael," gently and rhythmically can help sustain focus and attune to that angel's frequency. Similarly, incorporating soft, harmonic sounds or tones during the session creates a resonance that elevates the practitioner's energy, fostering an environment conducive to angelic presence. Such sounds act as an energetic invitation, a way of harmonizing the practitioner's energy with the angelic realms.

Occasionally, challenges arise—moments where messages feel unclear or the mind struggles to relax. In such moments, the practitioner is encouraged to maintain patience and humility, trusting that clarity will come when the time is right. It is common to encounter periods where the messages seem faint or elusive. Rather than forcing connection, the practitioner can reaffirm their intention, expressing gratitude and allowing the session to close naturally, with trust that future messages will emerge with greater clarity.

With time and dedication, channeling becomes a form of spiritual companionship, as the practitioner grows attuned to the presence of angels in more than just dedicated sessions. Signs, symbols, and impressions often surface spontaneously, bridging the channeling experience into daily life. In moments of quiet reflection or in times of need, the practitioner may feel the familiar presence of angelic guidance, knowing that communication is always accessible, transcending the boundaries of formal rituals.

Closing a session with gratitude, the practitioner offers thanks, acknowledging the angelic presence and their guidance. In doing so, they honor the sacred connection, fostering a space of mutual respect and continuity. As they express gratitude, the practitioner reaffirms their commitment to honoring and integrating the wisdom received, even if the message's meaning is not immediately clear. This closing gesture serves to complete the session with humility and grace, recognizing the partnership between human intention and angelic insight.

In this enriched relationship, channeling becomes a pathway to understanding one's higher purpose and the subtle ways angels support and guide. The messages received, often simple yet profound, weave into the fabric of daily life, inviting the practitioner to live with greater awareness, trust, and compassion. Through channeling, the practitioner finds themselves in continual dialogue with the angelic realms—a dialogue that transcends words and enters the heart, opening pathways to a life aligned with divine wisdom.

Chapter 24
Angelic Visions

Visions, as glimpses into the angelic realm, bridge the gap between the physical and spiritual, offering symbols, images, and sensations that extend beyond words. In these moments, the veil between worlds thins, allowing insights to surface in the mind's eye. Such visions are often layered with meaning, carrying messages that reveal themselves only through contemplation, an open heart, and a receptive mind. In the sacred process of receiving these visions, the practitioner begins to understand the subtle language through which angels communicate, a language woven from light, color, and sensation.

Preparing for an angelic vision begins with a state of deep relaxation and focused intention. Finding a quiet space, free from distractions, the practitioner centers themselves, breathing in a rhythm that grounds the body while lifting the spirit. As the mind settles, the practitioner might visualize a sphere of light expanding around them, a protective boundary through which only pure and positive energies can pass. This visualization creates a safe and inviting environment, setting the stage for angelic presence to be perceived in clear, gentle ways.

An invocation, spoken softly or held in thought, calls upon the angels to share their messages in a form that the practitioner is ready to receive. A simple request such as, "Angels of light, guide me with visions that reveal your wisdom," aligns the practitioner's intent with their openness to the visual language of the angelic. Once the invocation is made, the practitioner lets go of expectation, surrendering to the experience. This act of release is key, for visions often arrive unexpectedly—unbidden images, colors, or impressions that enter when the mind is still.

In the unfolding of a vision, the practitioner learns to observe without interference. Angelic visions are often soft and fleeting at first, emerging as faint glimmers of light, symbols, or ethereal figures. Rather than attempting to interpret the vision immediately, the practitioner simply observes, allowing each image or sensation to unfold. Some might see shimmering lights, colors, or forms that evoke a feeling of peace. Others may sense an angelic presence more strongly, such as a figure standing nearby, hands outstretched in a gesture of guidance or reassurance.

Colors hold particular significance in angelic visions, each shade resonating with a specific energy and message. For instance, golden light often conveys wisdom and protection, while blue light may symbolize healing or peace. White light is frequently a sign of purity and divine guidance. The practitioner begins to attune to these colors, recognizing them as aspects of angelic messages. Over time, they may notice patterns in the colors that appear, gaining insight into recurring themes or areas of life that angels are addressing.

Alongside colors, symbols are a central part of angelic visions, each carrying unique and often personal meanings. An open doorway, a path through a forest, or a gentle stream may appear, each representing guidance, transformation, or emotional healing. Angels communicate through archetypal symbols that resonate deeply with the practitioner's experiences and emotions. By noting these symbols and reflecting on their relevance, the practitioner finds meaning that goes beyond the visual, touching on themes that are woven into their own life journey.

At times, visions may also include sounds, fragrances, or sensations that deepen the experience. A soft melody, a scent of roses, or a feeling of warmth on the skin can accompany the vision, adding layers to the message. These sensory elements serve as anchors, making the vision more tangible and memorable. The practitioner may sense an elevated frequency in these moments, a subtle reminder that they are in the presence of angelic energy. Sensing these qualities enriches the vision, turning it into a multidimensional experience.

As visions grow clearer and more frequent, the practitioner learns to discern their personal meaning, recognizing that angelic visions are often deeply symbolic. After each vision, time is taken to reflect, capturing the experience in a journal. In writing, the practitioner can revisit each detail, noting the colors, symbols, and emotions that surfaced. This act of recording allows the practitioner to see recurring themes and patterns over time, a process that gradually reveals the layers of wisdom embedded within each vision.

Patterns in visions offer profound insights into the practitioner's spiritual journey. Recurring symbols—such as a winding path, an archway, or a radiant star—may emerge over multiple sessions, each iteration offering new layers of meaning. A symbol that initially appeared simple, like a feather or a candle, might take on added significance as it reappears, guiding the practitioner through phases of growth, healing, or transformation. In this way, angelic visions create a map of the practitioner's spiritual evolution, a map that becomes clearer with each experience.

Trusting these visions requires a delicate balance of openness and discernment. At times, the mind may question the authenticity of a vision, casting doubt on the experience. The practitioner learns to trust the subtle, peaceful energy that accompanies genuine angelic visions. A sense of inner calm, clarity, or lightness often signifies a true angelic encounter, helping the practitioner distinguish between the whisper of angels and the noise of personal thought. In cultivating this discernment, the practitioner builds confidence in the authenticity of the visions.

There may be moments when the practitioner encounters complex or enigmatic visions, images that are difficult to interpret or understand. Rather than seeking immediate clarity, the practitioner is encouraged to hold these visions gently, knowing that their meaning will reveal itself over time. Patience is essential, as angelic messages often unfold in layers, their full significance becoming apparent only as the practitioner's life journey progresses. This patient approach honors the gradual unveiling of divine guidance, allowing wisdom to emerge naturally.

After each vision, the practitioner closes the session with gratitude, a heartfelt acknowledgment of the angelic presence and the insights shared. In doing so, they honor the sacred exchange and invite continued guidance. Expressing gratitude, whether through words or quiet reflection, strengthens the bond with the angelic realm, keeping the channel open for future visions. This closing act is a gentle reminder that angelic guidance is a gift, an offering that enriches the soul and illuminates the path forward.

In time, the practice of receiving angelic visions becomes a source of comfort, strength, and insight. Each vision, a glimpse of divine presence, affirms the practitioner's connection to the angels and their support in all aspects of life. Through this sacred exchange, the practitioner not only receives guidance but also learns to view the world with new eyes, perceiving signs of angelic presence in the subtle beauty of everyday life. This evolving vision extends beyond ritual, becoming a way of seeing that brings the practitioner ever closer to the heart of divine wisdom.

With time, the process of understanding angelic visions deepens, revealing layers of insight that may not be immediately apparent. The ethereal nature of angelic symbols often defies direct interpretation, encouraging the practitioner to approach these visions with an open, curious heart. As each experience unfolds, subtle changes in how visions appear—their brightness, motion, or energy—provide important clues, allowing the practitioner to see not only the message itself but the deeper connection to the angelic realm.

The practice of engaging more fully with angelic visions begins by observing recurring themes. In these visual encounters, the practitioner may begin to notice patterns: symbols that arise frequently or colors that persist through several visions. Perhaps a golden light that suggests protection appears again and again, or perhaps an open doorway emerges, representing opportunity or guidance. These patterns carry profound meanings, often aligning with ongoing challenges, transformations, or decisions in the practitioner's life. By identifying these recurring symbols, the practitioner starts to discern how the angels are illuminating a personal spiritual path.

Visions at this level frequently contain messages that go beyond the visual, carrying sensations or sounds that further shape the experience. These multisensory elements are powerful guides, offering the practitioner a way to experience the message as a complete embodiment of angelic energy. For example, the image of flowing water may be accompanied by the soft sound of a stream, carrying a peaceful resonance that signals calmness or emotional cleansing. Recognizing these deeper aspects enables the practitioner to internalize the vision's wisdom fully, sensing not only its meaning but the emotional and spiritual state it evokes.

In this expanded practice, the practitioner also learns to meditate on their visions in the days following the experience, letting their meaning unfold naturally. Angelic messages can be layered, sometimes unveiling new insights days or weeks later, depending on the practitioner's readiness. Through quiet meditation, the practitioner returns to the vision, recalling its symbols and sensations, breathing life back into the images, and gently allowing further meaning to emerge. With each reflection, details that seemed minor—a certain color, a distant symbol—often become focal points of discovery, adding to the richness of angelic guidance.

Dreams, too, play a role in unveiling angelic visions, bridging the conscious and subconscious. As the practitioner develops sensitivity to these visions, they may notice that certain symbols or sensations surface in their dreams. Dreams can act as an extension of waking visions, providing further context or clarity to angelic messages. In this twilight state, the practitioner connects with the angels on a level unfiltered by the waking mind, allowing a pure flow of insight and reassurance. By maintaining a dream journal and noting recurring images or emotions, the practitioner weaves together a fuller tapestry of understanding, observing how angels continue to speak in the quiet hours.

Another powerful technique for integrating angelic visions is symbolic drawing or painting. By capturing the essence of the vision on paper or canvas, the practitioner reinforces their connection with the message, giving it form and color in the physical world. This creative process serves as a form of spiritual embodiment, grounding the vision's energy and allowing it to live beyond the moment of its appearance. The act of drawing or painting angelic symbols, even with simple lines or colors, enables the practitioner to process and reflect on the experience in a new way, blending artistic expression with spiritual insight.

In addition to creative practices, specific rituals can deepen the interpretation and integration of angelic visions. Simple rituals, such as lighting a candle while meditating on the vision's symbols or repeating a mantra that aligns with its message, anchor the vision in the practitioner's daily life. For example, if a vision contains a symbol of strength, the practitioner may light a candle each morning, setting the intention to carry that strength throughout the day. This repeated action acts as a reminder, reinforcing the vision's guidance and drawing the practitioner closer to its essence over time.

In these deeper experiences, the role of trust becomes even more significant. The practitioner may sometimes question the clarity or relevance of a vision, especially if its symbols seem unfamiliar or challenging to interpret. Here, the practitioner is called to trust that every vision holds purpose, even if its meaning remains hidden for now. Angels communicate in ways that resonate beyond logic, touching the soul's innate understanding. Through trust, the practitioner opens themselves to receive without judgment, knowing that each vision, however subtle, is an expression of divine presence meant to inspire, guide, or reassure.

There are also instances when a vision appears with a sense of urgency, offering a message that feels timely or essential. These visions are often clearer, marked by intense colors, heightened sensations, or an unmistakable feeling of immediacy. They may indicate moments of impending change or the need for caution and preparation. When these visions arise, the practitioner may feel compelled to take immediate steps in response, whether through prayer, meditation, or practical action. Such visions are reminders of the angels' protective role, guiding the practitioner to navigate their life's path with greater awareness and intention.

Over time, the practitioner builds a personal language of symbols, a unique lexicon through which angels communicate directly and consistently. A feather might come to represent divine reassurance, a star as a symbol of guidance, or a rose as a reminder of love and compassion. This language, deeply personal and intimately understood, becomes the practitioner's compass in spiritual navigation. Each vision speaks with familiarity and depth, resonating within the practitioner's life and aligning with their spiritual growth. In recognizing and honoring this symbolic language, the practitioner gains clarity, interpreting each new vision with an intuitive confidence that grows with every encounter.

As the practice evolves, angelic visions also provide opportunities for sharing wisdom. Sometimes, the practitioner may feel that a particular vision carries a message not only for themselves but for loved ones or their community. Guided by compassion, they may share the vision's insights, offering comfort or guidance to others. The act of sharing becomes a form of angelic work, an extension of the angels' love that reaches beyond the practitioner to touch those around them. By becoming a vessel for angelic wisdom, the practitioner's visions ripple outward, gently influencing the collective spiritual journey.

Ultimately, the continuous practice of receiving, interpreting, and integrating angelic visions becomes a transformative journey. Through each vision, the practitioner builds a relationship with the angels that feels like an unspoken, lifelong dialogue. The initial curiosity gives way to deep trust and reverence, and the visions become markers of personal growth, each one a step toward greater spiritual awareness. In these quiet moments of communion, the practitioner experiences the angelic presence as constant and unwavering, guiding them to perceive the world through a lens of light, love, and divine insight.

Chapter 25
Healing Rituals

In the gentle approach of healing rituals, the energy of angels begins to move in subtle, restorative ways. Angels have long been regarded as messengers and helpers, but within these ceremonies, they take on a new role—that of healers. These rituals call upon their nurturing energies to soothe physical, emotional, and spiritual wounds, restoring the harmony that often feels elusive in the human experience.

The act of seeking angelic healing starts with preparing the heart to receive this celestial support. There is a stillness required, a calming of the mind and an opening of the spirit to the soft, light-filled hands of these beings. This alignment is essential, for angels are attuned to the highest vibrations and respond most powerfully to purity of intent and the honesty of need. A gentle breathing exercise is often the first step, with each exhale releasing any tension, pain, or doubt, leaving room for the tranquil presence of angelic care to enter.

In these healing rituals, certain symbols and tools carry a unique power, acting as conduits for angelic energies. Crystals known for their calming and purifying qualities—such as amethyst, rose quartz, and selenite—are frequently included, each one chosen for the specific type of healing desired. Amethyst, for instance, is particularly effective in emotional healing, resonating with a calming purple glow that harmonizes the spirit, while rose quartz nurtures the heart and encourages forgiveness. The crystals are first consecrated with a simple prayer, perhaps by holding them close to the heart and asking the angels to infuse them with healing light.

To deepen the connection, an invocation is spoken aloud, calling specific angels known for their healing attributes. Archangel Raphael, often considered the angel of healing, is a frequent presence in these ceremonies. His emerald green light is visualized filling the space, touching every corner, and enveloping the practitioner in a shield of health and renewal. The invocation may be as simple as, "Archangel Raphael, guardian of healing light, bring your grace and restoration here. Allow your energies to flow into this space and into my spirit, restoring all that is weary."

Once this invitation has been extended, the practitioner focuses on the areas where healing is most needed, visualizing these parts of the self as open to angelic energies. The light of the angel, whether it appears as green, blue, or another comforting color, is mentally guided to the area, wrapping it in warmth and gentle pressure. Those with physical pain might sense this light entering sore or tense muscles, alleviating discomfort and infusing calm. For emotional wounds, the light may settle over the heart, softly working through past hurt, grief, or anxiety, replacing it with peace and a sense of protection.

To further enhance this ritual, the act of laying hands upon oneself can create a direct connection, allowing angelic energy to flow more directly. Placing hands on the heart, head, or other parts of the body symbolizes a release, a trust that healing will come from beyond oneself. In this quiet touch, there is a sense of returning to simplicity, a reminder of the self's worthiness of divine care and the body's innate wisdom to receive it.

Throughout the ritual, gratitude becomes a cornerstone of the healing journey. Even before any sensations of relief arise, the practitioner offers thanks to the angels, acknowledging their gentle efforts and their unwavering presence. This expression of gratitude elevates the vibration of the ritual, turning it from a mere act of seeking help into a sacred dialogue, a celebration of the bond between human and angelic beings. With each word of thanks, the practitioner strengthens their openness to healing, surrendering doubts and any lingering resistance.

As the healing ritual draws to a close, the practitioner is encouraged to place any burdens or unresolved pain into the hands of the angels, mentally visualizing this release. Whether it's a lingering sadness, a chronic worry, or physical ache, these are placed into the care of the angels, allowing them to carry away what is heavy. This simple act of handing over can transform even the most subtle resistance into an act of faith and trust.

A gentle closing prayer signifies the completion of the healing ritual, thanking the angels for their assistance and affirming trust in the healing process. This prayer may be spoken in a low voice or silently, with words as simple as, "I thank you, radiant beings of light, for your presence, your healing, and your love. I release all I have held tightly and open to your grace, knowing that healing flows freely and deeply." As these words settle in the heart, the practitioner is filled with the knowing that healing is continuous, moving and working in unseen ways long after the ritual ends.

In the hours or days following the ritual, the practitioner might feel subtle shifts, as though layers of tension or worry are gradually lifting. They may notice a sense of calm that feels deeper than usual, or moments of clarity in which past pains seem softened, their edges blurred by the gentleness of angelic touch. This is the work of angels, who move quietly, restoring the spirit from within, helping each part of the self to remember its divine origin and innate wholeness.

In the practice of these healing rituals, angels remind the practitioner of an essential truth: healing is not a destination but a journey, a gentle process that unfolds with time, compassion, and faith. Each ritual is a step along this journey, a moment of sacred connection that gradually leads the practitioner closer to inner peace and harmony. Through this consistent practice, the practitioner discovers that healing is a divine rhythm, a quiet song sung by angels that resonates in every cell, awakening a deep and lasting sense of wellness and love.

The depths of angelic healing reveal themselves through more advanced practices, guiding the practitioner to experience profound and transformative energies. Here, angelic support becomes a direct, intentional force capable of addressing specific conditions, both physical and spiritual. Each step of this ritual is like a chord, resonating and expanding in harmony with angelic frequencies, inviting a more profound healing to occur in a uniquely tailored way.

To begin, the practitioner settles into a space dedicated to stillness. Breathing becomes the first anchor, a gentle rhythm that draws the focus inward, where awareness of the body's needs becomes clearer. In this focused state, the practitioner starts with conscious breathing, allowing each inhale to invite angelic presence and each exhale to release any residual tension or doubt. A slow, steady breath opens the heart, mind, and spirit, preparing all aspects of being for the potent and sacred energy that is about to flow.

As the practitioner prepares to call upon angelic forces, they can choose to incorporate specific hand placements and visualizations. When invoking angels like Raphael or even guardian angels aligned with the healing purpose, positioning one's hands over an area of pain or imbalance can establish a more personal connection. Hands over the heart center invite emotional healing, while hands over the forehead help clear mental tension, opening pathways to a serene mind. This focused contact aligns the practitioner's intent with the angels' energy, reinforcing their bond and ensuring a deeper healing reception.

The visualization of light is central to these advanced rituals. As the angels are summoned, the practitioner imagines a sphere of brilliant, soothing light filling the space. The color of this light, often an emerald green for Raphael's healing or a soft blue for calming energies, surrounds and infuses the practitioner's body. The light is visualized as pulsing and flowing, a steady presence with the sensation of warmth and peace, moving into every cell and dissolving blockages. This healing light is felt as alive, flowing through the practitioner with precision and love, carrying a powerful, renewing force.

At this stage, conscious breathing is combined with visualization. On each inhale, the practitioner imagines drawing angelic light deep into their being, and on each exhale, they release any lingering discomfort or tension. This cyclical breathing is repeated until a rhythm of relaxation and openness develops. As light permeates, it flows to areas needing healing, whether an old injury or a painful memory, surrounding and penetrating the wound with angelic grace.

For specific conditions, this advanced practice introduces techniques of guided imagery. The practitioner visualizes the condition or wound as a shape or color within their body. Perhaps a tense area appears as a dark, swirling cloud or a rigid, dense form. With each breath and visualization of light, this cloud or shape begins to dissolve and transform, breaking apart under the gentle, persistent touch of angelic energy. It might disperse into tiny points of light, finally integrating with the body's natural rhythms and aligning with a state of calm and ease. This process not only addresses physical symptoms but invites the practitioner to release any emotions or thoughts associated with the pain, fostering a holistic sense of healing.

In these practices, intention is sharpened and focused. The practitioner speaks inwardly or outwardly, clearly articulating the desire for healing and openness. Words are like keys that unlock the inner doors, inviting angels to perform their work without obstruction. A simple, sincere intention may sound like, "I welcome angelic light to heal, restore, and bring peace to all aspects of my being," or, "Raphael, guide this healing energy to where it is needed most, transforming all pain into peace."

Another essential component is gratitude, woven into each part of the ritual. This expression is not only a closing gesture but an active part of the energy exchange between practitioner and angel. Gratitude amplifies the connection, increasing the power and effectiveness of angelic assistance. After sensing the angels' presence and light, the practitioner allows feelings of thankfulness to emerge naturally, an acknowledgment of this sacred union. It might take the form of a quiet prayer, a simple "thank you" to the angels, or a moment of silence where only gratitude is felt.

As the ritual concludes, a closing visualization grounds the energy received. The practitioner sees any remaining healing light anchoring into their body, residing within cells, bones, and spirit. They imagine this light becoming a permanent part of them, accessible at any time, a quiet glow that reinforces their health and well-being. To ensure stability, the practitioner grounds themselves with a final, calming breath and a visualization of roots growing from their feet into the earth, connecting to a solid foundation of peace and strength.

Over the coming days, subtle and lasting changes may unfold. The practitioner may feel a release from tension or an unexpected wave of calm. These shifts reflect the ongoing work of angelic energy, which, like a gentle river, flows in ways both immediate and mysterious, moving through layers of the self to bring about profound healing.

Through these advanced healing rituals, the practitioner learns to work alongside angels as partners, creating a space where healing is not merely an act but a deeply transformative journey. Each ritual reinforces that healing is a collaborative path, one that honors the wisdom of angels and the resilience of the human spirit, creating a bridge to continual peace, restoration, and spiritual harmony.

Chapter 26
Strengthening the Energy Field

Strengthening the energy field is a journey of self-protection, expansion, and resilience, a practice that invokes angels to create an aura fortified against the weight of external influences. In this space, we recognize that our personal energy can be strengthened through the gentle, yet powerful, guidance of angelic forces. Just as a flame needs oxygen and fuel to keep burning, the energy field around us needs regular nourishment and intentional reinforcement to remain resilient and pure.

This practice begins with a mindful awareness of the personal energy field, sometimes felt as a warm or tingling sensation surrounding the body. The practitioner starts by tuning into this sensation, recognizing its subtle texture and boundaries. With closed eyes, they picture their energy field as a light-filled aura encompassing their entire body, gently pulsating with their heartbeat. This visualization forms the foundation, a reminder of the powerful energetic presence each person naturally holds.

To call upon angelic assistance in strengthening this energy field, a quiet invocation is spoken, requesting guidance and protection. An invocation to Archangel Michael, the angel of strength and protection, is a common approach, as his energy is often described as a shield of brilliant, radiant blue light. With focus and reverence, the practitioner might say, "Archangel Michael, I invite your presence to fortify my energy field, to fill me with strength and unwavering protection." This call opens the space for angelic support to infuse the personal aura with resilience and a powerful sense of calm.

Visualizations deepen this connection. As the practitioner breathes deeply, they envision a sphere of protective light enveloping them, dense yet gentle, glistening with shades of blue and white. Each inhale brings the sphere closer, while each exhale strengthens it, solidifying its presence around them. This sphere acts as a sacred boundary, filtering energies that approach, allowing only love, peace, and light to pass through.

To intensify this practice, a powerful tool lies in the use of specific angelic symbols and affirmations. The practitioner can visualize symbols like a radiant shield or a flaming sword—often associated with Archangel Michael—as a means to further solidify the protection. These symbols, glowing with light, are visualized encircling the energy field, warding off any dense energies. Each affirmation strengthens this intent: "I am surrounded by divine light, safe and protected in the angelic presence." These words, repeated silently or aloud, anchor the visualization in a deeper conviction, creating a palpable sense of strength within the practitioner's energy field.

Incorporating crystals amplifies this process, their unique vibrations aligning with angelic energies to create a more robust aura. Crystals like black tourmaline, known for its grounding properties, or clear quartz, for its amplifying nature, are ideal for this practice. Holding a crystal, or placing it near the body, the practitioner envisions its energy merging with their own. The crystal acts as a stabilizer, its frequency intertwining with the personal aura to enhance resilience and clear away any lingering tension or lower energies.

Regular practice of this ritual becomes a profound way to maintain the clarity and vibrancy of one's energy. The practitioner learns to check in with their energy field frequently, noting when it feels dense or heavy and choosing practices to cleanse and recharge it. Over time, this awareness becomes an instinctive protection, a way to remain grounded and secure even amidst external chaos.

A final key to strengthening the energy field lies in grounding techniques, which anchor the fortified energy within the practitioner. After visualizing the protective aura, they picture roots extending from their body deep into the earth, connecting to a vast reserve of strength and stability. This grounding links the energy field to a constant source of energy, helping to maintain its fortification and prevent exhaustion. The practitioner feels a sense of completeness and confidence as they stand connected both to the earth below and the angelic realm above.

Through this practice, the energy field becomes more than just a protective barrier—it transforms into a dynamic extension of the self, alive with angelic light and strength. The practitioner, now more attuned to their energy and its needs, finds a new level of resilience and peace, assured in the knowledge that their aura, strengthened with angelic support, is a sanctuary of unwavering protection.

As the energy field grows more resilient, the practitioner learns to cultivate a sense of harmony and heightened awareness, refining the energetic shield through a series of advanced practices. This stage delves into integrating angelic symbols and tools into daily routines, nurturing a connection that makes protection a constant companion. Through consistency and devotion, the energy field becomes not just a barrier against negative influences, but a luminous aura that naturally attracts peace, joy, and spiritual clarity.

A morning practice is a foundational technique in maintaining this fortified energy field throughout the day. Upon waking, the practitioner visualizes a sphere of angelic light, vibrant and translucent, enveloping them from head to toe. This shield can be infused with a specific angelic color according to need—gold for strength, blue for protection, or white for purity. They allow the color to radiate outward, pulsating with every breath, establishing an aura of calm strength that will sustain them in all encounters.

To deepen this protective practice, crystals can be incorporated for their unique vibrations, amplifying the energy field's resonance. By carrying a crystal like amethyst or smoky quartz, the practitioner can keep their energy balanced and grounded. Each morning, holding the crystal and visualizing it filling the aura with its vibration, they program it with their intention. A simple affirmation such as, "I am protected and grounded," repeated with focus, binds the crystal to their purpose, making it a constant ally in maintaining a powerful energy field.

Throughout the day, maintaining awareness of the energy field becomes a natural and instinctive process, aligning thoughts and actions with the intention of preserving harmony. Before entering crowded or high-stress environments, the practitioner reaffirms their shield by envisioning the angelic light intensifying, and silently calling upon the angelic guides to strengthen its layers. A brief moment of deep, slow breathing allows them to feel this angelic reinforcement, creating a peaceful buffer zone in challenging surroundings.

The visualization of specific angelic symbols around the aura is another potent method for continual protection. The practitioner may imagine symbols like a circle of angelic crosses or radiant stars forming around the energy field, shimmering with angelic light. Each symbol reinforces the aura with its energy, creating a pattern that not only shields but also raises the field's frequency, acting as a magnet for positive experiences and interactions. This visualization can be done in moments of meditation or as a quick reminder during the day.

Nightfall brings another opportunity to cleanse and strengthen the field, clearing any residual energies gathered during the day. A simple yet powerful practice is to light a white candle before bedtime, symbolizing a purification of the personal space. In the candle's glow, the practitioner visualizes any unwanted energies dissipating, leaving their aura bright and renewed. With a prayer or an invocation to their guardian angel, they invite a calming, angelic presence to wash over them, preparing for restful, spiritually protected sleep.

Incorporating gratitude further enhances the energy field's strength, building a relationship of continuous reciprocation with the angels. By closing each day with a moment of thanksgiving, the practitioner acknowledges the guardianship and blessings received. This gratitude might be expressed silently or through a simple prayer: "Thank you, beloved angels, for your presence and protection. May my heart remain open and my spirit aligned with your light." This practice, though small, cultivates a deeper bond with the angelic realm, naturally strengthening the energetic shield through a sense of trust and divine connection.

In time, these daily rituals transform into a seamless part of life, each day an opportunity to refine and nourish the personal energy field with angelic support. This continual fortification becomes an invisible yet powerful presence, a shield of light that adapts and grows alongside the practitioner. Through conscious daily choices and connection with angelic guidance, the energy field evolves into a vibrant sanctuary, a constant source of strength and inner peace.

Chapter 27
Ritual for Requests

The act of formulating a request to the angelic realm is both delicate and powerful, carrying within it the weight of true intention. As one stands on the threshold between the human and the divine, each word chosen for a request shapes the energy that reaches the angels. Guidance here explores the art of making clear, thoughtful requests that align with the heart's deepest needs and aspirations, inviting a response that is equally precise and supportive.

To begin, the practitioner must reflect on the nature of their request. Before asking anything of the angels, one must explore the heart's motivations with honesty. Are they seeking guidance, healing, protection, or clarity? This clarity of purpose is essential, as the angelic realm responds most powerfully to intentions that resonate with authenticity. A period of quiet meditation allows the practitioner to connect with their inner self, centering the mind and spirit in a calm, receptive state where intentions become clear and focused.

Once the intention is defined, it's crucial to choose the right words with care and respect. Angels, as messengers of divine wisdom, respond to requests that carry the vibrational frequency of respect, love, and gratitude. With this in mind, the practitioner might begin their request with a phrase like, "Beloved angels of light, I call upon your guidance and wisdom…" or "Gracious guardians, I humbly seek your assistance…" Speaking in a way that acknowledges their spiritual nature opens a channel that is both respectful and inviting, creating an atmosphere of trust.

Visualizing the request can deepen its impact, particularly when clarity is required. As the practitioner formulates their words, they envision their request in the form of a radiant light, perhaps taking the shape of a symbol or object that represents the essence of their desire—a blooming flower for growth, a flame for clarity, or a shield for protection. This visualization imprints the request in the practitioner's own consciousness while simultaneously sending it out into the angelic realm with vivid intention.

As the request is sent, silence becomes an important component of the ritual. In this silence, the practitioner listens—not necessarily for immediate answers, but for the subtle changes in energy or emotion that arise within. This silence invites the angels' response to come in its own time and form, nurturing a patient and receptive mindset. Sitting with hands open, or palms resting gently on the heart, the practitioner embraces a posture of openness, signifying willingness to receive whatever guidance or insight may come.

The ritual of making a request to angels benefits from consistency, as the angels may choose to communicate answers through gentle signs over days, or even weeks. Simple daily practices that keep the intention alive, such as lighting a candle each morning or repeating a short affirmation, reinforce the connection. "With gratitude, I am open to the wisdom of the angels" can be whispered as a reminder of the request, echoing the practitioner's ongoing trust in the process.

Gratitude, too, is essential in concluding each request, not just as an expression of thanks for future guidance, but as an affirmation of faith in the journey itself. A moment of gratitude after the request, even if answers have not yet arrived, creates a foundation of humility and respect. The practitioner might say, "Thank you, gracious angels, for hearing my heart," acknowledging the presence of angelic support, trusting that guidance is already on its way, even if unseen.

At the heart of any request lies the courage to ask and the patience to await a response, nurturing a dialogue that transcends words. Each request made, each whisper of the heart, contributes to a relationship that grows deeper and more intuitive. Through this process, the practitioner learns that in asking, they are also opening themselves to the subtle, transformative power of divine love and wisdom, their spirit moving closer to the resonance of angelic light.

As the act of making requests to angels unfolds, the journey reveals itself not merely as a path of asking, but as one of trust, patience, and the silent cultivation of a deep, abiding faith in unseen forces. Guidance here explores how to deepen the art of request-making through practices that nurture patience and align the seeker with the rhythms of divine timing. It invites the practitioner to strengthen their connection with angelic wisdom by weaving gratitude into each step of the process, creating a gentle, continuous dialogue with the angelic realm.

In approaching any request, the practitioner is reminded to hold their intentions with openness rather than urgency. Angels often respond to our heart's intentions in subtle, unexpected ways, arriving like a breeze rather than a storm. This openness is nurtured through a quiet understanding that the wisdom of the angels may offer guidance that diverges from initial expectations. To cultivate such trust, the practitioner can use affirmations like, "I trust in the timing of the divine," or "I am open to the path the angels reveal." These affirmations calm the heart, allowing space for angelic responses to appear in their own form and time.

Visualizations and meditative practices play a key role in sustaining alignment. A useful technique is to visualize oneself surrounded by a soft, radiant light, symbolizing the steady and unwavering presence of the angelic realm. This light can be seen as a gentle cocoon, providing reassurance and holding the practitioner in a space of acceptance and faith. Each time a request is revisited, the practitioner allows themselves to breathe into this light, reaffirming that they are supported, even if answers remain elusive for a time.

Additionally, acts of gratitude amplify the connection with angels, infusing the ritual of requesting with a profound sense of reverence and peace. Gratitude in this context is more than polite acknowledgment; it is a vibration that rises from the heart, amplifying the energetic connection with angels. Each time the practitioner thanks the angels, they signal their faith in the process, regardless of the immediacy or clarity of response. They might express, "I am grateful for your presence in my life," or "Thank you for guiding me in ways I may not yet understand." This form of gratitude deepens trust and creates a harmonious flow between the seeker and the angelic realm.

Throughout this process, the practitioner may encounter moments of doubt or impatience, especially if the answers they seek do not arrive in expected forms. These emotions are natural and can be transformed into growth points on the spiritual path. When doubt arises, the practitioner can place their hand over their heart, taking a few mindful breaths, and silently acknowledge, "I release my need for immediate answers; I trust in the wisdom that unfolds." Such moments of self-compassion allow the practitioner to reconnect with the essence of angelic trust.

A journal dedicated to recording both requests and any signs received can be an invaluable companion on this journey. By documenting dreams, synchronicities, or subtle intuitions, the practitioner starts to perceive patterns in angelic responses over time. This journal becomes a tapestry of angelic dialogue, offering insights into how the angels communicate uniquely with each seeker. It is often through such records that the practitioner can look back and recognize how angelic guidance has subtly influenced their path, perhaps without their immediate awareness.

One of the most profound lessons in request-making is the realization that sometimes the angels answer in ways that are not direct solutions, but rather gentle nudges towards inner growth or unseen opportunities. In cultivating patience, the practitioner discovers that the journey of connection itself holds immeasurable value. They come to understand that in seeking the angels' wisdom, they are also deepening their relationship with their own spiritual essence, learning to listen with both heart and spirit.

Over time, the seeker's heart becomes attuned to the subtleties of divine guidance, perceiving even the faintest whisper of angelic presence. With each request made, each moment of patient waiting, they learn to dwell in a space of peace, fortified by the presence of angelic light. This peace is the ultimate response, the gift of patience, the gentle reminder that the angels are, indeed, always near, guiding and loving in the background, illuminating the soul's path with quiet constancy and care.

Chapter 28
Personal Spiritual Journey

The journey into one's spirit is deeply personal and constantly unfolding, often in ways that elude immediate understanding. Here, angels act not only as guides but as luminous companions on a path marked by self-discovery, inner challenge, and awakening. To embark upon the spiritual journey with the assistance of angels is to step into an experience where layers of self are revealed and transformed, often beginning subtly, with moments of recognition or flashes of insight that feel like gentle whispers from beyond.

Each step of this journey invites the seeker to cultivate a relationship with their angels that is at once sacred and deeply attuned to their inner world. For angels, the work of guiding is more than simply offering advice; it is an endeavor to help the practitioner unveil their highest truths. They accompany us not by pointing out all answers but by stirring the deeper questions that encourage growth and alignment with one's soul purpose. Methods are revealed to listen to these questions as they arise, to sense the angelic nudges toward one's unique spiritual path, and to approach each experience, pleasant or challenging, as a stepping stone on the way to enlightenment.

Rituals, both simple and profound, help anchor these experiences. For those seeking to bring angelic guidance into their spiritual journey, the daily practice of setting an intention each morning can be a powerful act. With a simple invocation, such as, "Angels of wisdom, be with me as I walk today's path; guide me toward understanding and strength," the practitioner sets the tone for their day with openness and respect for the mysteries that may unfold. Throughout this journey, there is no single right way to move forward, but there is always a way of walking with attentiveness, honoring the experiences as they come.

As the practitioner progresses, they may begin to notice recurring signs, symbols, or feelings that seem to speak directly to their inner life. This could manifest as an affinity for certain symbols or numbers, specific messages in dreams, or an unexpected clarity that arises in moments of solitude. Angels often use these gentle signs to communicate, helping the practitioner to feel connected to the unfolding journey. A journal to record these symbols, dreams, or any intuitive messages can serve as a meaningful touchstone, allowing the seeker to reflect on the guidance received and witness the patterns in their own transformation.

To deepen this experience, meditation becomes essential. The seeker is encouraged to create a space within themselves where they may tune in to angelic presence without distraction. Through meditative practices that focus on visualization, such as envisioning a path of light stretching into a boundless horizon, the practitioner can attune their senses to angelic frequencies, opening their heart and mind to the subtle language of spirit. Here, the angels are felt not just as guides but as silent companions, walking beside the seeker and illuminating the way forward.

Over time, the practitioner may feel an urge to seek clarity about their spiritual purpose. This longing is natural and speaks to the soul's desire for alignment with divine truth. Angels can help clarify this purpose, though they often do so by stirring an awareness that arises gently and organically rather than through direct answers. The seeker is encouraged to trust this process, to allow their purpose to reveal itself layer by layer, like petals opening in the warmth of the sun. In these moments, the practitioner may find peace in asking, "What is my purpose here, angels of light?" and simply remaining present with whatever sensations, emotions, or thoughts emerge.

During the more challenging moments on this journey, when the path seems unclear or self-doubt creeps in, the angels offer a steady presence. This presence is both grounding and expansive, reminding the seeker that they are never alone, even in times of difficulty. The practice of calling upon specific angels for strength or insight during these moments can provide reassurance and guidance. For example, one might invoke Archangel Michael for courage, Raphael for healing, or Gabriel for clarity, allowing these archangels' energies to help the practitioner stay connected to their inner truth, even when external circumstances feel overwhelming.

Ultimately, the spiritual journey is one of continual self-discovery and transcendence, a dance between the seeker and the spirit world, with angels as trusted companions.

As the spiritual journey deepens, the presence of angels becomes increasingly vivid, guiding the practitioner not merely through signs but through experiences that shape inner understanding and foster spiritual resilience. Each step forward on this path is a call to refine intuition, to trust one's own insight as it unfolds, and to explore the soul's purpose with a courage that is both gentle and unwavering. Guidance here seeks to expand the relationship with angels as companions and mentors, exploring the subtle layers of their guidance, which is felt not only through signs but through the echoes of wisdom that arise in moments of quiet contemplation.

With each experience, the practitioner learns to interpret the delicate language of symbols, emotions, and visions that often carry angelic messages. These messages may come in dreams or be woven into the tapestry of everyday life, where an unanticipated kindness or a moment of clarity reveals a greater understanding. The key is to remain attuned, to perceive not only with the mind but with the heart. Angels often reach us in ways that defy logic yet resonate deeply within, urging us to listen closely and without the interference of doubt.

To cultivate this openness, the practitioner may incorporate rituals that create a sacred space for angelic communion. Evening rituals, for instance, can serve as a quiet anchor for reflection, encouraging the practitioner to revisit their day and recognize moments of angelic presence. With a candle lit, the practitioner can hold a simple intention, such as, "Angels of insight, help me understand my path," allowing thoughts, emotions, or memories to rise, and reflecting on what these may signify. This gentle practice of attunement builds a vocabulary of the heart, enabling the practitioner to interpret angelic guidance with increasing clarity and trust.

As this journey progresses, angels may present guidance in ways that challenge the practitioner to confront their own shadows or face personal truths that may have been buried. Angels do not shield us from these aspects of growth but instead offer the strength to move through them with grace. In these moments, the guidance from angels serves to remind the practitioner that every obstacle on the path has its purpose, each difficulty a teacher. Invoking one's guardian angel during these times of personal reckoning can bring comfort and assurance, as if feeling a light hand on the shoulder, grounding the seeker in courage and clarity.

To deepen trust in angelic guidance, the practitioner can practice intentional surrender—an active release of one's attachment to specific outcomes. This surrender is not a passive act but rather a conscious decision to accept guidance from a place of deep faith, acknowledging that the angels may see beyond what we can presently understand. The act of saying, "I am here, open to receive your wisdom," creates an internal openness that invites messages to arrive in surprising and profound ways. Through surrender, the practitioner learns the sacred balance between effort and allowance, acting with intention yet remaining open to the unknown.

Journaling also becomes a profound tool for deciphering the threads of angelic communication. This practice allows the seeker to document dreams, insights, and signs, to weave them together and uncover patterns that may reveal a broader narrative or direction. By reflecting on these entries over time, the practitioner may observe recurring symbols or themes that form a map of sorts, guiding them forward with each entry. Angels often work through the subtle repetition of themes, and journaling creates a space for these messages to come together, revealing the wisdom that emerges when we connect each moment to a larger, unfolding story.

Trust in angelic wisdom grows in quiet steps, often through repeated experiences of synchronicity or by feeling an unmistakable sense of alignment in particular decisions. When seeking guidance for specific choices on this journey, the practitioner may visualize a council of angels encircling them, their presence as luminous guardians radiating support and clarity. In this space, the seeker may ask a direct question and allow answers to form, whether through intuitive knowing, feelings, or gentle shifts in thought. Each response, however subtle, is an affirmation that this guidance is real and available, a truth that becomes more evident as the seeker continues.

Over time, the spiritual journey transforms from a quest for understanding to an embodied experience of connection with the angelic realm. This unity brings peace that is deeply internal, resonating in each moment and choice. As the seeker strengthens their relationship with angels, they begin to feel a merging of their personal path with the flow of divine intention, each step a dance with guidance, each challenge a reminder of the strength they carry within. The journey is one of continual return to this inner light, a light that angels help to kindle and keep aflame, leading the seeker toward the full realization of their purpose and potential.

Chapter 29
Angelic Wisdom

The path of angelic wisdom unfolds as a journey of subtle revelation, where insights are given not as directives but as seeds planted in the heart and mind, awaiting their moment to take root and flourish. Angelic wisdom is less a list of instructions and more a quiet, continuous guidance that calls for trust, patience, and an open spirit. This exploration delves into the transformative nature of angelic wisdom and how it can be woven into the fabric of everyday life, serving as a compass for inner harmony, clarity, and purpose.

Angels impart wisdom not in loud declarations but in whispers that seem to emerge from within. Their messages often carry a sense of recognition, as if they arise from a place of deep inner knowing. This wisdom flows naturally when the practitioner practices stillness, allowing the mind to settle and the heart to expand. Simple moments of reflection, such as pausing to listen to one's breath or observing the quiet rhythms of nature, open pathways for this inner wisdom to emerge. Angels guide us to pay attention to these seemingly mundane experiences, as each carries the potential to reveal profound truths.

Living by angelic wisdom involves adopting a gentle, mindful presence throughout daily life, remaining aware of how each thought, action, and decision aligns with one's inner values and spiritual goals. This awareness becomes a spiritual practice in itself, a form of moving meditation where every moment is infused with presence. By asking oneself in small, intentional ways, "How would I act with the wisdom of angels?" the practitioner begins to integrate higher principles into their day-to-day decisions. In this way, angelic wisdom ceases to be something external or distant; it becomes an intrinsic part of one's own perspective and choices.

The guidance of angels often invites the practitioner to recognize the subtle layers of experience—to see beyond surface appearances and connect with the deeper essence of people and situations. Angels teach that each person carries within them their own journey, their own truths, and that approaching others with compassion and non-judgment honors the divine within them. As one practices seeing through the lens of angelic understanding, judgments soften, and a space for genuine compassion opens, transforming relationships and interactions.

In moments of confusion or uncertainty, angels encourage the practitioner to turn inward rather than seek external answers. Angelic wisdom reminds us that clarity is often found in stillness, that within each of us lies a wellspring of insight waiting to be tapped. By practicing mindfulness, by consciously breathing and allowing thoughts to settle, the practitioner can listen to the deeper layers of intuition, where the angels' guidance is heard more clearly. In these spaces, angels gently remind us of our strengths, our inherent wisdom, and our connection to the divine.

Incorporating angelic wisdom also involves the willingness to let go of the need for immediate answers or perfect solutions. Angels often impart wisdom that challenges us to accept ambiguity, to recognize that true insight can evolve and deepen over time. In this way, angelic wisdom is not a rigid framework but a fluid, evolving understanding that allows the practitioner to grow, adapt, and refine their path. This wisdom encourages flexibility, an openness to change, and a trust in the unfolding of one's journey, knowing that the angels are there, illuminating each step, even if the destination remains unseen.

The practice of gratitude becomes a vital part of integrating angelic wisdom. Each day, expressing gratitude for the guidance received, for the moments of peace and clarity, and for the presence of angels in one's life, strengthens the connection to this wisdom. Gratitude creates an energetic alignment with the angelic realm, reminding the practitioner to remain receptive and humble. Whether through a quiet prayer, a written reflection, or a simple "thank you" whispered to the angels, gratitude amplifies the flow of wisdom, anchoring it in the practitioner's heart and mind.

As one continues to live by angelic wisdom, an intuitive sense of alignment emerges—a feeling of being in harmony with oneself, with others, and with the greater flow of life. This harmony does not eliminate challenges or hardships, but it transforms the practitioner's approach to them. Obstacles are met with resilience, and setbacks become opportunities for deeper understanding. The practitioner learns to perceive life's complexities with grace, guided by the sense that each experience, however difficult, holds a lesson infused with divine intention.

In the end, the journey with angelic wisdom is one of self-discovery, a gradual unveiling of the soul's unique path and purpose. It is an invitation to live from a place of love, humility, and connection, to allow the wisdom of angels to illuminate the inner landscape of the heart and mind. This wisdom, as it becomes integrated into daily life, transforms every moment into a sacred experience, bringing the practitioner ever closer to the realization of their spiritual essence and their place in the tapestry of creation.

The deeper path of angelic wisdom invites the practitioner to embrace an even greater level of attunement to the subtle messages, insights, and energies that angels impart daily. Further guidance explores how to cultivate a continuous state of awareness, recognizing angelic guidance not only in moments of meditation or ritual but within the very fabric of daily life. The practice of living by angelic wisdom becomes a lifelong journey, a harmonious dance between spiritual alignment and earthly experience.

Angelic wisdom flourishes in spaces of openness and humility, where the practitioner learns to listen beyond words and perceive beyond appearances. It is in this receptive state that the smallest, simplest experiences reveal unexpected layers of meaning. Whether in moments of silence, nature, or the unspoken exchanges with others, angels guide us toward an understanding of life that is both expansive and deeply personal. To practice this wisdom is to see each moment as an invitation to understand oneself and others more compassionately, to meet life with an open heart and a steady mind.

Central to integrating angelic wisdom is the art of observation without attachment. Angels encourage us to witness our experiences without immediately assigning labels or judgments, allowing thoughts and feelings to rise and fall as naturally as the breath. Through this process, the practitioner begins to recognize patterns within themselves—cycles of thought, emotions, or reactions that, once observed without judgment, reveal their roots and meanings. This is the foundation of angelic wisdom: to witness oneself with the same nonjudgmental clarity and kindness that angels offer.

Through mindful observation, the practitioner also begins to see how angels subtly influence their intuition, often nudging them toward choices that align with their higher self. This guidance, though gentle, becomes clear when the practitioner is attuned to it, recognizing the sense of ease and inner peace that accompanies angelic influence. Angels teach that their wisdom rarely manifests as dramatic revelation; instead, it appears as a soft, consistent pull toward authenticity, kindness, and patience. As the practitioner follows these gentle inclinations, they cultivate trust in their intuitive sense, which gradually strengthens their connection to angelic wisdom.

Anchoring this wisdom in daily life requires intentionality and practice. One way to nurture this is by dedicating moments each day to reflect on one's thoughts, actions, and emotions with honesty and openness. Whether through journaling, silent reflection, or intentional breathing, these practices provide a space where the wisdom of angels can be acknowledged and absorbed. This ritual of self-reflection is not meant to be complex; rather, it is a simple act of presence, a willingness to pause and listen, allowing the subtle layers of angelic guidance to reveal themselves.

As this wisdom deepens, the practitioner becomes increasingly aware of the ripple effects of their actions, understanding that even the smallest gesture holds significance. Angels encourage us to act with love and respect, to move gently in the world, as these actions resonate in unseen ways. When acting from a place of wisdom, one becomes a vessel of light and peace, subtly impacting those around them. Angels remind us that wisdom is not only about the self but about our interconnectedness with all beings. Living this wisdom, the practitioner becomes a silent beacon of angelic grace, embodying kindness, patience, and understanding.

To sustain this deepened wisdom, angels encourage practices of alignment and gratitude. Practicing gratitude daily strengthens the energetic bond with the angelic realm, drawing angelic presence closer into one's life. Each day, whether by silently acknowledging the blessings one receives or by expressing thanks to the angels in quiet prayer, gratitude opens the heart, making it receptive to angelic insight. By thanking the angels for their presence, wisdom, and guidance, the practitioner cultivates a resilient channel of connection, one that withstands even life's most challenging moments.

In maintaining a balanced perspective, angelic wisdom reminds us of the importance of grounding—staying rooted in the present moment even as one's spirit expands. Angels teach that true wisdom resides in the harmony between the earthly and the divine, where one honors their humanity while recognizing their spiritual essence. To ground this balance, the practitioner may find value in practices such as mindful walking, spending time in nature, or focusing on the breath to anchor themselves. This grounding enables the practitioner to experience angelic wisdom without losing touch with the realities of the physical world.

Angels also encourage the practitioner to honor cycles of growth and rest, to recognize that wisdom is a journey, not a destination. There are times of clarity and times of uncertainty, times of action and times of stillness, and angelic wisdom is present in all phases. By embracing these natural cycles, the practitioner learns to release the need for constant progress, understanding that every moment, even the quiet ones, contributes to their spiritual growth.

In closing, angelic wisdom is both a gift and a practice—a continuous unfolding that brings the practitioner into deeper resonance with their highest self. This wisdom is not confined to rituals or meditations but becomes a way of being, a quiet alignment with love, compassion, and peace. As the practitioner lives in harmony with this wisdom, they embody the angelic qualities they have come to revere, finding that the divine is not a distant presence but a living force within their own heart and soul. Through this journey, the practitioner and the angels walk together, united in purpose, ever aligned with the timeless rhythm of the divine.

Chapter 30
The Circle of Light: Protection and Spiritual Strengthening

A Circle of Light, created with angelic presence, offers a powerful shield of protection and a source of spiritual empowerment. This sacred circle surrounds the practitioner with divine energy, forming an invisible boundary that purifies, strengthens, and safeguards. Within this space, the energies of the angels can flow freely, creating an atmosphere that is deeply secure and spiritually potent, ideal for both personal reflection and interaction with the angelic realm.

To create a Circle of Light, the practitioner must approach the ritual with clarity of purpose and respect for the sacred energies being called. This ritual begins with a grounding breath, drawing one's awareness inward, centering both body and mind. With each breath, the practitioner releases any residual worries or distractions, opening a pathway to the presence of angels. A simple prayer, a reverent acknowledgment of angelic protection, helps to signal one's readiness to enter this sacred space.

The practitioner may then imagine a radiant light—a bright, soothing energy—emanating from their heart or crown, expanding outward in all directions. This light grows into a sphere, encircling them, creating a radiant boundary. This boundary becomes the Circle of Light, an enclosure infused with the purity and strength of angelic energies. It is essential to hold an intention of protection and harmony, inviting the angels to stand as guardians within and around the circle.

While envisioning this light, the practitioner may feel the presence of specific guardian angels or sense a general warmth and calm that signifies their closeness. Visualizing the circle with intention, one can focus on its properties: it is a barrier against negativity, a place of renewal, and a channel for angelic support. As the light strengthens, the practitioner becomes attuned to a sense of profound security, knowing that within this space, they are under the angels' direct protection and influence.

The power of the Circle of Light does not come solely from the practitioner's visualization but is magnified by the angels who answer the call for protection. Each angel brings unique qualities to the circle. Some bring warmth, others a feeling of clarity or joy. Archangels, too, can be invited into this space, each contributing their particular protective strengths. Archangel Michael, known for his powerful shielding energies, often becomes a sentinel for those seeking defense against negative influences or spiritual exhaustion. In this way, the practitioner's intentions harmonize with angelic attributes, creating a tailored, impenetrable light that both guards and uplifts.

Within this circle, the practitioner can seek to release unwanted energies and emotional burdens, knowing they will be cleansed by the angelic forces at work. Simply breathing within the circle can release tension, fears, or fatigue. As these energies dissolve, the practitioner may experience a sense of lightness, even joy, as the angels transmute dense energies into something finer and more radiant. In this process, the Circle of Light serves not only as a shield but as a transformative, nurturing space where one's spirit can renew and expand.

The strength of this circle lies in its adaptability, allowing it to respond to specific needs. For example, in times of significant change or personal challenge, the circle can be reinforced with an additional layer of protection by repeating the visualization, using verbal affirmations, or calling on multiple angels. Words spoken within this space carry power, and simple statements like "I am protected and strengthened by the light of the angels" enhance the practitioner's alignment with the circle's purpose. Through such affirmations, the practitioner weaves their own energy into the angelic framework, creating a deeply personalized bond.

The Circle of Light becomes a reliable refuge, a place the practitioner can revisit frequently, whether through meditation, moments of stress, or daily routines. Over time, with consistent practice, the boundary of the Circle of Light may become instinctive—a sensation that the practitioner carries even beyond formal rituals. The constant presence of angelic protection then becomes second nature, offering comfort and a sense of stability in various environments.

Beyond personal use, the Circle of Light can also be extended to encompass loved ones, one's home, or spaces in need of energetic uplift. By visualizing the light expanding outward, enveloping family members, friends, or a specific area, the practitioner creates a field of angelic support that serves as a blessing and a shield. While the effects of this extension vary based on need and intention, the foundational protection remains, offering safety and peace to all within its reach.

As one strengthens this practice, the Circle of Light becomes not just a means of protection but a bridge to spiritual empowerment. Within its boundary, the practitioner can set intentions, meditate, or seek guidance from angels, knowing they are in a safe and pure space. This empowerment nurtures a sense of spiritual sovereignty, reminding the practitioner that, in partnership with angels, they can create and sustain spaces of peace and light within themselves and their surroundings.

In closing, the Circle of Light ritual is both deeply personal and infinitely adaptable, a testament to the enduring strength of angelic protection. It requires no elaborate preparation, only a sincere heart and clear intention, and yet it offers profound benefits—shielding the practitioner, transforming energies, and opening a channel for angelic interaction. It becomes, in essence, a living bond between the practitioner and the divine forces of light. In moments of need or quiet reflection, the Circle of Light stands as a reminder of angelic presence, a radiant sanctuary that offers protection, guidance, and unwavering support.

Once the Circle of Light is established, it becomes a practice of enduring strength, a sanctuary that grows in resonance with each use. Guidance explores the process of deepening and fortifying the circle, transforming it into a lasting source of connection with the angels. By reinforcing the circle over time, the practitioner learns to maintain its protective qualities, adapting it to different life situations or challenges, making it an ever-present shield of light and peace.

To reinforce the Circle of Light, one must first return to the intention that underpins it. The practitioner begins by invoking the angels with a sincere heart, expressing gratitude for their continued presence and protection. With each invocation, a greater sensitivity develops, strengthening the relationship with the angels and heightening awareness of the circle's energetic boundaries. The practitioner can feel this protection as a tangible sensation—perhaps as warmth, a gentle pressure, or even as a sense of heightened clarity.

Visualization plays a crucial role in maintaining the circle's strength. By imagining the light as vibrant and alive, constantly pulsing with energy, the practitioner establishes a dynamic boundary that responds intuitively to changes in energy or circumstance. With each breath, the light circle can be "fed" with renewed strength, radiating a deeper, more resilient energy. This pulsating light becomes attuned to the practitioner's needs, a barrier that grows stronger with each intentional practice.

An additional technique for fortifying the circle is to introduce sacred symbols or angelic sigils within the visualization. Specific symbols—such as a radiant cross or an angelic eye—can be visualized hovering within the circle, serving as both protection and as a point of focus for deeper meditation. These symbols act as reminders of angelic presence, infusing the circle with layers of spiritual meaning and further embedding the intention of safety and light. Just as a gemstone can be programmed with intention, these symbols become conduits of amplified protection.

Regular rituals of blessing, where one formally recharges the circle, can also strengthen its potency. In these sessions, the practitioner may choose to use specific mantras or words of power, like "I am safe, I am guarded, I am at peace," as they mentally affirm the circle's inviolable nature. With each repetition, a rhythm of confidence and reassurance builds, turning the words into a kind of spiritual armor. By speaking aloud, the practitioner unifies mind, body, and spirit, cementing the circle as an active force of protection.

In moments of particular vulnerability, the practitioner can call upon archangels for added reinforcement. Each archangel, when invoked, brings their unique qualities into the circle, offering specialized forms of guidance and protection. Archangel Michael, for instance, lends courage and resilience, enveloping the practitioner with his powerful blue flame of defense. Gabriel, in turn, contributes clarity and wisdom, creating an atmosphere where fears and doubts dissipate. Through the presence of these archangels, the circle becomes a fortress of light, each angelic energy interwoven into the practitioner's own intentions.

The circle can also be adapted as a communal practice, extended to include family, friends, or spaces in need of light. Through visualization, the circle's boundary can be widened, embracing homes, work environments, or even loved ones. The practitioner visualizes the circle expanding like a dome of light, enveloping others in a serene glow of protection and peace. This broadened circle not only shields those within but creates a harmonizing effect, promoting unity and calm. In times of difficulty, this expanded circle serves as a beacon, inviting angelic presence to protect and uplift all who are embraced by it.

Over time, this practice of extension and reinforcement leads the practitioner to experience the Circle of Light as an enduring presence. There is no longer a need to consciously invoke it in every instance; rather, the circle becomes embedded within their energy field. Even in challenging situations, where fear or doubt might arise, the practitioner feels the silent strength of the circle, like an aura of angelic protection surrounding them. This continual presence brings not only security but a subtle, ongoing attunement to the angelic realm.

The power of the Circle of Light lies in its adaptability, a sacred protection that grows and transforms with the practitioner's journey. Each strengthening ritual, each invocation, becomes a step toward spiritual resilience. Within this light, there is an unspoken understanding—the practitioner is never alone, for angels stand guard, silent and vigilant. The circle itself becomes a testament to their connection, a sanctuary within which the practitioner can find peace, insight, and healing at any moment.

As the practitioner integrates this awareness into their daily life, the Circle of Light becomes more than just a ritual of protection; it is a reminder of the angelic presence that infuses all things, a gentle yet powerful assurance that divine energies flow through and around them, guiding and shielding each step of the journey.

Chapter 31
State of Union with Angels

The path to union with angels invites the practitioner beyond ritual and invocation, guiding them to a place of silent communion, where angelic presence becomes an innate part of their essence. This journey toward spiritual union is less about calling forth angels and more about dissolving the boundaries that separate the self from the divine, allowing angelic light to permeate the soul's very fabric.

The journey begins with meditation as a doorway into this union, not as a practice to reach out but to look within, where the energies of angels resonate subtly. In quieting the mind, breathing becomes the anchor, each inhale drawing in light, each exhale releasing barriers. Over time, the breathing slows, and a vast stillness takes hold—a state of receptivity in which the practitioner no longer waits for messages but rests in the peace of simply being with angelic energies. This silence becomes rich with presence, as if each heartbeat pulses with angelic love, and each breath nourishes with divine assurance.

A vital part of this practice is learning to perceive angelic energy as a subtle inner light, an ethereal glow sensed rather than seen, its warmth felt in the chest or as a gentle radiance surrounding the body. This light is angelic essence—a direct communion experienced within, where words and thoughts fall away. As the practitioner attunes to this presence, an innate recognition arises, a knowing beyond intellect, in which they feel the distinct qualities of angelic love, strength, and serenity.

Visualization aids in deepening this union. Here, the practitioner no longer envisions an angel outside themselves but allows a soft, golden light to expand from within, filling every cell and reaching out into the spaces around them. This inner light merges with the angelic realm, its boundaries dissolving as it spreads. In this radiant expanse, the practitioner experiences a sense of oneness with the angelic, realizing that they too carry this light, that they, in essence, are of this same divine source.

This state of union brings transformative shifts in perception. The practitioner finds a heightened sensitivity to subtle energies in daily life—whether in nature, in silence, or in the presence of others, as if angelic grace now flows quietly through each encounter. Emotions, too, align to a gentle rhythm, where anger softens, sorrow lifts, and love flows more freely. A new clarity arises, a wisdom that seems to come from beyond oneself, guiding actions and responses. In this way, the practitioner is no longer reaching out to angels; they are moving in harmony with them, navigating life with an angelic insight and compassion.

Trusting this connection is key. The practitioner learns to rely not on external validation but on an inner resonance, a quiet certainty that the angels are not only near but within, ever-present in the very core of their being. There are no grand gestures or visions needed—only a steady, unshakeable knowing that one is supported, seen, and loved by forces that transcend time and space.

As union deepens, certain practices help to reinforce this connection, enabling the practitioner to carry angelic awareness throughout daily life. A simple act of mindful breathing, for instance, serves as a reminder of this unity. With each inhale, the practitioner draws in light; with each exhale, they release any thoughts or worries that separate them from this awareness. In moments of challenge or doubt, this breath becomes a lifeline, anchoring them in the serenity of angelic presence.

Silent prayer also deepens this state of union. Unlike invocations or requests, this form of prayer is a wordless offering of the heart, an openness to angelic wisdom and love that requires nothing in return. In this quiet surrender, the practitioner feels a profound peace, a divine alignment in which their desires and fears dissolve, replaced by a gentle acceptance. This prayer does not ask for guidance; it becomes guidance, a trust in the perfection of angelic support in all moments.

Through these practices, the practitioner begins to sense a continuous, abiding connection with angels, transcending formal rituals. The need for invocation, for specific words or gestures, becomes less necessary, for angelic presence is felt constantly, an invisible force woven through every thought, every interaction. The practitioner moves through life enveloped by this unseen light, aware that they are never alone, that the angels dwell not only around but within them.

In the moments of union, there is a profound humility that arises—a reverence not only for angels but for the sacredness in all beings, for each carries this same divine essence. The practitioner sees the light of angels reflected in others, perceiving their struggles and joys with a compassion that transcends judgment. This state of grace transforms everyday life into a continuous act of devotion, a silent service to the divine presence shared by all.

As the guidance unfolds, the practitioner is encouraged to embrace the simplicity of this union. To be at peace in silence, to walk with an open heart, to breathe as one with angels—this is the essence of the spiritual union. There is no need to seek grand experiences or proof, for the proof lies within, in the gentle but constant presence that guides, uplifts, and heals from within.

In this union, the practitioner finds not only communion with angels but a profound reunion with their true self, the essence that transcends form and embraces divine light. The angelic realm is no longer a distant place to reach; it is here, now, an inseparable part of their journey, the quiet foundation of their being. And with each passing day, as the awareness of this union grows, life itself becomes a sacred prayer, a continuous song of gratitude and love for the angels that walk beside and within them.

As the union with angels deepens, the practitioner discovers how to maintain this connection even amidst life's inevitable challenges. This state of union is not confined to moments of meditation or rituals; rather, it becomes a steady presence, a spiritual foundation that gently permeates every aspect of existence, especially when faced with uncertainty or inner turmoil. Through refined practices and unwavering trust, this bond becomes an unbreakable source of peace and guidance.

In times of inner conflict, the practitioner is encouraged to seek stillness and breathe deeply, allowing angelic light to rise within. This breathing becomes an act of surrender, inviting divine support to soothe anxiety and realign thoughts and emotions. With each exhalation, the practitioner releases fears, doubts, and the mental noise that clouds clarity, welcoming the calm embrace of angelic peace. This steadying practice does not aim to erase difficulties but rather to illuminate a higher perspective from within the soul. Slowly, a sense of acceptance fills the heart, a subtle shift that allows the practitioner to view challenges with an open, calm gaze.

Visualization further strengthens this state, transforming it into a constant source of resilience. The practitioner can call upon the image of angelic light surrounding them, creating a protective shield that becomes a quiet reminder of the divine support that always accompanies them. In moments of stress or uncertainty, they close their eyes, envisioning a brilliant sphere of light enveloping their being, radiating warmth and strength. This visualization becomes not only a form of protection but also a grounding presence that brings forth clarity, helping the practitioner to move forward with renewed perspective and courage.

Additionally, maintaining this inner connection through small, sacred rituals woven into daily life is emphasized. Simple actions, such as lighting a candle, pausing in gratitude, or even taking a moment to gaze at the sky, serve as reminders of angelic presence. These rituals need not be elaborate; their power lies in the intention behind them. When the practitioner approaches each of these moments with a quiet heart and open spirit, they amplify the angelic presence within and around them, making their life a living testament to divine harmony.

Guided journaling offers another method to anchor this union, especially during moments of doubt or confusion. By writing down feelings, thoughts, and questions, the practitioner opens a channel through which angelic insights can flow naturally. This practice is not a search for direct answers but a means of clearing the mind, allowing wisdom to emerge from a place beyond conscious thought. As the practitioner reflects on their writings, subtle patterns and insights often reveal themselves, offering clarity and perspective that were previously hidden.

In maintaining this union, the practitioner also learns to cultivate a state of compassionate detachment. This does not mean withdrawing from life's emotions or challenges but rather embracing them with the awareness that they are part of a larger spiritual journey. With each experience, whether joyful or sorrowful, they become an observer as well as a participant, viewing their life with an angelic perspective that transcends judgment. This compassionate detachment allows them to feel deeply without becoming entangled, to face trials with grace, and to respond to others with unconditional love and understanding.

Perhaps the most profound aspect of sustaining this state of union is the inner transformation it brings. As the practitioner grows closer to angelic energies, they begin to reflect these qualities in their own actions and choices. Compassion becomes a natural response, wisdom flows effortlessly, and a quiet strength radiates from within. There is no need to strive for these qualities—they emerge spontaneously from the heart's growing alignment with divine presence. In this way, the practitioner not only feels connected to angels but becomes a living vessel of their light and love, carrying angelic grace into every interaction and situation.

Over time, this union fosters an expanded awareness that reaches beyond the self. The practitioner begins to sense the interconnectedness of all beings, recognizing a shared divine essence that unites them with others and with the world at large. This sense of unity brings a profound responsibility, an understanding that their thoughts, words, and actions resonate far beyond their immediate sphere. With this awareness, they move through life with a heightened sense of reverence, knowing that each moment is a sacred opportunity to embody the angelic qualities of love, kindness, and peace.

In sustaining this union, gratitude becomes a cornerstone of the practitioner's journey. They cultivate a practice of silent thanksgiving, not only for blessings received but for each opportunity to learn, grow, and serve. This gratitude extends beyond prayer or ritual, becoming an attitude of the heart. Through this constant thanksgiving, the practitioner keeps the channels of divine connection open and vibrant, inviting angels to remain close as ever-present guides on their path.

The guidance concludes with a practice of inner quietude—a simple yet powerful exercise that invites the practitioner to rest in the silence within. In this silence, free from expectations or desires, they experience the fullness of angelic presence. There are no words, no images—only the sensation of being cradled in light, of dissolving into the divine energy that pervades all. This quietude is not a goal to be achieved but a state to be allowed, a space where the practitioner meets the angels in a communion that transcends form, a place where they recognize themselves as part of the angelic essence.

Through this journey of union, the practitioner no longer seeks angelic guidance as something external. They realize that this connection is a reflection of their own divine nature, a sacred resonance that exists within. With each breath, each step, they carry this light, this love, into the world, serving as a bridge between the angelic realm and the earthly, embodying a peace that is as infinite as the angels themselves. In this state of sustained union, life itself becomes a luminous offering, a quiet, constant celebration of the divine in all things.

Chapter 32
Concluding the Cycle

In the quiet culmination of this journey, a deeper understanding begins to settle within, like the steady glow of a distant light growing closer. The cycle has brought the practitioner full circle, from the first cautious steps of reaching out to angels to a place of profound union and trust. Now, as they reflect on each ritual, meditation, and invocation that guided them along this path, an inner knowing arises: the work is not ending; it is transforming, carrying forward as a part of the practitioner's essence, as constant as breath.

The connection with angels, once perceived as an external guidance, has revealed itself as an ever-present aspect of the practitioner's inner world. This realization brings a new depth to their relationship with angels—not one defined by rituals alone, but by a state of openness that permeates daily life. This awareness brings a quiet joy, an understanding that angels are not only there in moments of prayer but walk beside them in every moment, in every breath, in the pauses and unspoken words, as natural as a heartbeat. This silent companionship transforms every action, thought, and feeling into a gesture of spiritual alignment.

Gratitude emerges as the first and perhaps most essential expression in this closing phase. The practitioner is encouraged to revisit the practices of gratitude taught along the way, seeing them anew as the foundation of their ongoing relationship with the angelic realm. With each act of gratitude—whether a whispered prayer, a simple moment of reflection, or a spontaneous offering of thanks—a bridge is renewed between the practitioner and the divine. This gratitude no longer serves merely as a ritual gesture; it becomes the language in which the soul speaks, the way the practitioner aligns and harmonizes with the subtle currents of angelic presence.

The journey taken is now contemplated, with each practice of connection, meditation, symbol, and sign seen as reflections of the deeper qualities the angels sought to awaken within the practitioner. This is a time for honoring the path as a sacred map, one that led them not only toward the angels but inward, toward their own divine self. With each ritual, the practitioner recognized facets of their soul—its peace, strength, and limitless capacity to connect. Now, with this map in hand, they move forward with trust, knowing that these qualities remain with them always.

Looking back, the practitioner finds that even the simplest acts—lighting a candle, saying a prayer, breathing in presence—have become intimate portals to the angelic realm. Through these small gestures, they have come to understand that no elaborate ritual is needed to reach angels, for angels dwell in the quiet spaces of the heart, in the silent intention behind each act. This realization deepens their approach to life itself, transforming ordinary moments into sacred encounters.

As a final act of gratitude and closure, the practitioner is encouraged to create a personal consecration ritual, an offering that marks both an end and a beginning. In a quiet, intentional space, they may light a candle, say a simple prayer, or lay out symbols that hold meaning from their journey. This ritual is a chance to offer thanks for the presence of angels, for their guidance and companionship, and to affirm the practitioner's commitment to carry forward this light in their own life. This ritual need not be elaborate—its beauty lies in sincerity, in the openness with which it is offered. As the practitioner concludes, they feel the weight of the cycle lifting, replaced by a renewed sense of purpose and peace.

Stepping into daily life with an awakened sensitivity to angelic whispers, they are encouraged to remain alert to the subtle signs and symbols that continue to appear, to trust the intuition that has strengthened throughout this journey. In moments of doubt, they remember that angels respond not only to grand invocations but to the simplest needs and sincerest questions, as near as thought itself. This awareness brings a quiet confidence, a trust that the support and wisdom of the angels are always within reach.

Through this cycle, the practitioner has woven an invisible thread of connection with angels that stretches far beyond ritual or prayer. This thread is woven into the fabric of daily life, guiding their choices, softening their interactions, and radiating a gentle peace that extends to those around them. This presence becomes a light that others feel—a quiet comfort that uplifts and inspires, even without words. In this way, the practitioner not only deepens their own connection with the angelic realm but becomes a living example of that connection, a reminder of divine love and guidance in the world.

A simple yet profound reminder closes this cycle: the journey with angels is never truly complete. Each encounter, each prayer, each quiet moment spent in their presence deepens the connection, opening new insights and revealing new layers of peace. The practitioner learns to trust this unfolding, allowing it to enrich their life as they continue forward. With every step, they carry the wisdom and light gained, a perpetual cycle of learning and growing closer to the divine essence within.

As the light of this journey shines softly, the practitioner stands in a state of reverent simplicity. There is nothing more to seek, nothing to strive for, only a gentle invitation to walk forward with an open heart. This is the quiet beauty of the angelic path: it begins anew with each moment, each breath, carrying the practitioner toward an ever-deepening harmony with the divine and with all beings. In this sacred union, they find not an end, but an infinite beginning, an eternal invitation to walk with the angels in peace.

With the cycle nearing its full completion, the practitioner now stands at a point of profound integration. In the silence and stillness that follow the final rituals, a deepened clarity begins to take root. The countless steps, invocations, and meditations are no longer separate practices; they are woven together into a living, breathing part of the practitioner's essence. Every lesson, each whispered guidance from the angels, and all the subtle signs encountered have merged into a cohesive whole that permeates their awareness.

At this juncture, the practitioner is invited to enter a final ritual of thanksgiving—a moment to honor the entire journey and the wisdom it has unveiled. Here, they might reflect on the beginnings of their path, recognizing the quiet transformation that has unfolded. The connection to the angelic realm is now part of their inner landscape, familiar and comforting, no longer something reached for, but a constant, reliable presence that feels as close as a heartbeat.

The thanksgiving ritual is simple yet profound. In a space that holds meaning—whether by the altar created, under the open sky, or in the quiet privacy of the heart—the practitioner is encouraged to offer an expression of gratitude to the angels for their guidance, protection, and unwavering companionship. This ritual, an intimate culmination, can be as elaborate or as unadorned as they feel drawn to create. A candle lit with intention, a prayer spoken from the soul, or a moment of silence—each gesture embodies an acknowledgment of the journey taken and the blessings received. The beauty of this final offering lies not in its form but in the depth of sincerity with which it is given.

After the thanksgiving, the practitioner enters a phase of consecration. This consecration represents a dedication, a vow to carry forward the light and insights gained into every facet of their life. Here, they might place a hand upon their heart, affirming an intention to embody the angelic qualities of love, peace, and compassion in their actions, words, and thoughts. It is a reminder that the journey does not end with the final page; rather, it continues as a radiant thread woven through daily life, lifting and inspiring all that they touch.

In this consecrated state, a new awareness emerges. The practitioner senses the gentle current of angelic presence extending not only to guide their own path but to offer comfort and peace to others. They understand now that, in aligning with the angels, they have become a vessel through which angelic energies flow—a beacon of hope and tranquility to those who may feel adrift. As they carry this light forward, they honor the angels not through words or rituals alone, but through a life that reflects their kindness, wisdom, and compassion.

This closing phase encourages the practitioner to embrace a daily rhythm of quiet reflection. Each day offers a new beginning, a fresh opportunity to reconnect with the angelic guidance within. Through brief moments of gratitude, simple acts of kindness, or pauses for silent prayer, the practitioner nurtures the ongoing bond with the angels. This rhythm of reflection serves not as an obligation but as a natural expression of their inner harmony, a gentle reminder of the unseen presence that accompanies every step.

As they walk forward, the practitioner is reminded of the angels' subtle language—signs in nature, a quiet nudge of intuition, an unexpected sense of peace in moments of doubt. These delicate whispers become cherished companions, ways in which the angels continue to share their guidance long after the structured rituals have concluded. Through these moments, the practitioner remains in dialogue with the divine, continuously attuned to the angelic wisdom that flows into the fabric of their life.

The journey's final teaching lies in the realization of unity, of a seamless connection between the practitioner and the angels that no longer requires words, symbols, or specific practices to sustain. It is a shared silence, a resonance that needs only the stillness of the heart to be felt. This unity brings an inner peace, a trust that transcends circumstance, illuminating the path forward. In this quiet, sacred union, the practitioner understands that the angels are with them in every choice, every interaction, each breath.

This closing of the cycle is not an end but a deep and steady beginning. The practitioner now walks with an open heart, perceiving the angelic presence as an integral part of life itself. With each day, they carry forward a radiant awareness, an unbreakable bond with the angels that serves as a source of light and strength. The journey, which began with curiosity and reverence, has unfolded into a profound state of being, where the practitioner is both guided and guiding, both held and holding—a living testament to the sacred partnership with the angelic realm.

And so, with this final consecration, the practitioner steps forward, forever marked by the grace and wisdom of this path. They walk in peace, embodying the angelic presence in all that they are, a quiet yet powerful force of compassion, courage, and serenity in the world.

Epilogue

Reaching the end of this reading, the path of angels and the call of light now feel more familiar. A journey has been completed, but it does not end here. What you hold are fragments of a greater truth, the introduction to a world you now understand more intimately. The angels, these beings of light accompanying the flow of creation, do not bid you farewell as these pages close; rather, they remain with you, now integrated into your field of perception, reminding you of the sacred that surrounds you.

The journey of your soul is an ever-evolving work, and angels, invisible guides and silent friends, accompany you in this unfolding. The knowledge you have gained here is not to be retained as mere information but to be lived and experienced. Each symbol, each concept, is a seed that, when it blossoms in your heart, expands your ability to perceive and embrace the divine around you. The world is no longer the same for one who has allowed themselves to see beyond, who has dared to feel the subtle touch of angels and embrace the truth of their own existence.

Now, equipped with this wisdom, you may perceive how your journey was never solitary. In every moment of sorrow, in each instance of doubt, there was an invisible support—a presence holding you. Angels are the manifestation of the love that permeates all things, the divine presence that walks by your side, offering guidance and support. They do not merely observe but actively participate, always respecting your free will and waiting only for a heartfelt call to intervene in subtle yet transformative ways.

May this journey awaken in you a trust in the unseen, in what transcends common perception. The signs you now recognize clearly—the fallen feather, the repeated number, the gentle breeze that suddenly surrounds you—are reminders of this alliance. And beyond this, may this connection inspire you to look upon the world with a new sensitivity, for the sacred manifests itself at every moment, waiting for the eyes of the soul to recognize it.

Angels are also keepers of memory and destiny, guarding the past and weaving futures that honor each soul's purpose. In every encounter and lesson, their presence reminds you that, although the path is personal, it is intrinsically connected to the whole. The changes you desire for the world begin in you, and the angels remind you that the peace, love, and truth you experience in moments of meditation and prayer can be mirrored in daily life.

Thus, as you conclude this reading, the angelic journey continues in your daily life. With each choice, each gesture, the universe conspires for your soul to blossom and grow, perfectly aligned with the greater plan that the angels guard and nurture. May you continue with an expanded heart, embracing the gifts that the spiritual world offers and keeping alive the flame of connection with the divine.